Highland inspiration

by

Rev Jim Lamont

HIGHLAND INSPIRATION

Designed and published by Impacto Print and Design, graphic design, colour and commercial printers, Unit C8, Enterprise Business Park, Lisnennan, Letterkenny, Co Donegal on behalf of the Highland Inspiration committee.

All proceeds in aid of Donegal Hospice, Letterkenny.

Cover pictures: Front cover: Mount Errigal, the highest peak in Co Donegal.
Rear cover: Falcarragh beach.

Photographs by Stanley Matchett and Sammy Wasson

ISBN-13 : 978-0-9551659-0-0

Contents

FOREWORD

Thought For The Day on my Highland Breakfast radio programme is designed to be a short spiritual message from members of the clergy or laity for listeners to take with them through the rest of the day. Just because it is religious is not a guarantee that people will pay heed, and therefore the aim is to capture the listener's attention and keep them engaged for the duration of the two-minute item.

It works best when the broadcaster leaves people pondering the message within that day's "Thought" and one man who has over the years really managed to capture the imagination of our listeners is the Rev Jim Lamont.

His simple stories are delivered in a relaxed tone and strike just the right note at 8.15am. Listeners know they are going to be able to grasp exactly what he is saying. They know that the story will be rounded off with a moral and that the Rev Jim will relate it succintly, in a non-preaching manner, to everyday life.

The reaction has been enormous and now the often asked question of: "Where can we get a copy of Jim Lamont's Thoughts for the Day?" is finally being answered.

The Rev Jim's contributions have been a real asset to the programme over the years and I hope this long overdue book will also give listeners a better appreciation of the man behind the voice. It gives me great pleasure to write this foreword and I commend this book to you, the reader.

JOHN BRESLIN
Presenter
Highland Breakfast

ACKNOWLEDGEMENTS

Highland Inspiration is an idea that was waiting to happen. Over the past six years, many listeners to Highland Radio have been impressed by the lucid, easily digestible yet profound Thoughts for the Day put out on air by the Rev Jim Lamont. There was a widespread feeling in Co Donegal and beyond that these broadcasts deserved a wider circulation in a more tangible form and that they should be gathered together in the form of a book for this purpose.

After some persuasion, Jim Lamont himself agreed that there was merit in the idea and so in March 2005 a small committee came together in Dunfanaghy to pursue the project. My fellow committee members were Sammy Wasson of Impacto Print in Letterkenny, whose company designed and published the book with such painstaking care and considerable toil, Jason Hunter, treasurer of Dunfanaghy Presbyterian Church, who diligently handled all the sponsorship cheques and ensured that our books balanced, Charlie Robinson from Dunfanaghy whose local knowledge and business contacts proved invaluable and JO Anderson, a holiday home owner and semi-retired accountant whose business acumen came to the fore. I owe them all a tremendous debt of gratitude. This has been a genuine team effort.

I should also like to take the opportunity of expressing sincere appreciation to many other people who made the dream of publishing this book become a reality. Isobell Doherty, the office administrator of Donegal Hospice, has been a source of encouragement and assistance over many months. Charlie Collins, managing director of Highland Radio has embraced the idea of the book from the outset, and has given valuable support. John Breslin, the presenter of the breakfast programme in which Thought for the Day is incorporated, has been an enthusiastic backer of the project, and has given us the benefit of his own experience of the book publishing world.

Stanley Matchett, a talented Belfast-based freelance photographer who runs residential courses for budding photographers at Arnolds Hotel in Dunfanaghy, gave generously of his time and expertise in shooting pictures for the book. To him and his partner Maureen Hunter, many thanks. Norman and Sheila Johnston of Colourpoint Press in Newtownards gave me much advice on the book publishing scene, and kept us right on several key issues.

I am grateful to Patricia McBride of An Grianan in Letterkenny for providing the theatre as a venue for the book launch in October 2005. And thanks must also go to the various support groups of the Donegal Hospice for their willing co-operation in the marketing of the book.

But none of this would have happened had it not been for the generosity of the sponsors who came forward with funds to cover the cost of producing and launching the book. They bought into the project, quite literally, and I trust that we have justified their leap of faith. I am pleased to report that we were able to cover all our overheads and to produce a small surplus which will go to the Hospice.

The names of the sponsors are listed in alphabetical order on another page of this book. To each and every one of them I say thank you. Without your support this book would not have been possible, and Donegal Hospice would have been deprived of valuable funding.

But my chief word of appreciation must go to the author, the Rev Jim Lamont, whose communication skills were the germ from which this book evolved. I know that his broadcasts are already eagerly anticipated and well received by his legion of listeners on Highland. I hope now that his powerful message will receive an even wider audience and trust that this book may serve to encourage, inspire, comfort and reassure all those who care to read through its pages.

ROBIN MORTON
Highland Inspiration committee convenor
Belfast, September 2005

DONEGAL HOSPICE

For more than a decade, a palliative care home-care service has been provided by the Donegal Hospice. This has now been augmented by the opening in February 2003 of the Donegal Hospice building in its own grounds at Knocknamona Road in Letterkenny. This facility has six bedrooms and two larger apartment areas. People are admitted under three criteria:

    (1)   symptom management

    (2)   respite care

    (3)   terminal care.

An average length of stay in the hospice is 14 days but this can be shorter or longer depending on the patient and family needs. Services are provided by a multi-disciplinary team which includes medical/nursing staff, occupational therapist, physiotherapist, home-care nursing provided by the community palliative care sisters and hospital support provided by the clinical nurse specialist palliative care team based at Letterkenny General Hospital. We also have the support of bereavement counsellors and social workers as needed. Other very important members of the team are the volunteers who provide complementary therapies of hairdressing and beautician skills.

Securing adequate finance is always a challenge and without generous support from the public, it would be difficult to maintain the present service. We remain deeply grateful to so many members of the public for their ongoing support.

I have quite deliberately left the involvement of the Presbyterian chaplain, the Rev Jim Lamont till last. Jim, who is responsible for this book, is a valued member of our team. When a person and their family are faced with a serious illness their spiritual care, irrespective of denomination, is of paramount importance. We are blessed and privileged at Donegal Hospice to have a team of chaplains who provide an exemplary service. They not only provide support and friendship for the patients and families but also for all staff and volunteers involved with the hospice. Without them, a major and important link in the chain would be missing.

I would especially like to thank Jim Lamont who has put together this beautiful book of thoughts, the proceeds of which are going to the Donegal Hospice.

LUCY McGETTIGAN

Nurse Manager

Donegal Hospice may be contacted at 074-9177256.

INTRODUCTION

Although the contents of this book were originally meant just for the radio, I have been persuaded - or perhaps cajoled - to put a selection of "Thoughts" that have been broadcast on Highland Radio in print. These thoughts have grown out of personal experiences or stories I have read and collected over the years. I believe that story telling is a most effective means of communication and this is the method I have found to be most helpful in putting together the Thoughts for the Day.

Ninety seconds isn't all that long to get a message across, so the story becomes the starting point out of which develops a single thought which hopefully listeners can take with them into the rest of the day. I do hope they may be of some help and encouragement to those who now read them.

I wish to thank the staff of Highland Radio for all the help and support I have received and also for the opportunity to broadcast "Thought for the Day" which I have been doing regularly for almost six years. Thanks to all those who have taken time to listen and to those who have written or phoned with their words of thanks and encouragement.

The generosity of our sponsors has meant that all the proceeds from the sale of the book will go to help in the invaluable work of the Donegal Hospice. It is an honour for me to act as Presbyterian chaplain in the Hospice and also in Letterkenny General Hospital, and to witness the dedication and devotion of the medical teams and other staff. I thank all the staff for their support and friendship and also all the other chaplains for their support, fellowship and good humour. I also express my appreciation to my two congregations of Carrigart and Dunfanaghy for both their practical and prayerful support over these years.

I don't believe anything ever happens in life without those who often work quietly and sometimes not so quietly in the background. So I thank Robin Morton for his drive and enthusiasm, along with his support staff of JO Anderson, Jason Hunter, Charlie Robinson and our publisher Sammy Wasson (Impacto Print) and everyone else who made this project possible.

Finally to my wife Anne and my family I simply say thank you!

REV JIM LAMONT
Dunfanaghy
September 2005

THE AUTHOR

The Rev Jim Lamont was born in Ballymena and was brought up on a farm outside the town. He is married to Anne and they have four children all of whom are married. They have nine grandchildren.

After several years teaching Rural Science Mr Lamont became a student for the ministry of the Presbyterian Church in Ireland. On the completion of his studies and an assistantship in Malone Presbyterian Church in Belfast, he became minister of the congregation of First Ballynahinch, then of Regent Street, Newtownards and for the past six years he has been the minister of the congregations of Carrigart and Dunfanaghy in Co Donegal.

Photo: Stanley Matchett

As well as being minister of these two congregations he also acts as Presbyterian chaplain to Letterkenny General Hospital and to the Donegal Hospice.

For almost six years he has been involved as one of the regular religious broadcasters on the Letterkenny-based independent radio station, Highland. He is a regular contributor to the "Thought for the Day" slot on John Breslin's breakfast show, as well as acting as one of the presenters of the Monday evening "Travelling with God" programme.

Mr Lamont's interests include amateur dramatics, computers, travel and a life-long passion for Manchester City football club, which must say something about his optimistic outlook on life!

One of Mr Lamont's recurring themes is that of the grace of God, which reaches out to us when we least deserve it. As recipients of such grace he believes that the Christian life should not stop at the church door; instead Christians should reach out in grace to engage with the community and address the wider needs and problems of the individual and of society. Over the years, he has given a message of hope to many people and continues to do so, both from the pulpit, within the local community and from behind the microphone in the broadcasting studio of Highland Radio. Long may the green light be illuminated!

ROBIN MORTON

Donegal Hospice in Letterkenny

The Rev Jim Lamont shares a thought with Dr. David Flanagan and Hospice Nursing Manager Lucy McGettigan

John Breslin and the Rev Jim Lamont get ready for another broadcast

Photo: Stanley Matchett

Carrigart Presbyterian Church

Photo: Stanley Matchett

Dunfanaghy Presbyterian Church

ALL THINGS ARE POSSIBLE

During the Thirty Years' War in the 17th century, a German pastor Paul Gerhardt and his family were forced to flee from their home. One night as they stayed in a small village inn, homeless and afraid, his wife broke down and cried openly in despair. To comfort her, Gerhardt reminded her of the promises found in the Bible about God's strength and presence. Then, going out to the garden to be alone, he too broke down and wept. He felt he had come to his darkest hour.

Soon afterward, Gerhardt felt the burden lifted and sensed a new the Lord's presence. Taking his pen, he wrote a hymn that has brought comfort to many. *"Give to the winds thy fears; hope, and be undismayed; God hears thy sighs and counts thy tears; God shall lift up thy head. Through waves and clouds and storms He gently clears the way. Wait thou His time, so shall the night soon end in joyous day."*

When life proves difficult and when darkness seems to be all around us so often it is then that God begins to feel so much closer to us. That was what the Psalmist experienced in his own life when he walked through the deep dark valleys; that he was not alone for God was with him.

God comes into the darkness of our sufferings and our sorrows and shows us that He is for us as the writer of the 46th Psalm expresses it: *"Our refuge and strength, an ever present help in times of trouble."* When we like Paul Gerhardt personally come to understand and to know this then we receive new hope.

It may be as you are reading this that you are facing great difficulty in your own life. Take heart. Put yourself in God's hands today and He will give you peace, strength and a future that is alive with hope.

There is no such thing as a hopeless situation; there are only people who have grown hopeless in the situation.

Take with you today those words of Jesus himself as we find them recorded by Matthew in his *Gospel: "With man this is impossible, but with God all things are possible."* (Matthew 19:26 NIV)

DON'T LOSE YOUR WONDER

A little girl was travelling on a train with her father. As she looked out the window, she saw many things that excited her. "Look daddy," she would exclaim, "there's a horse ... Look daddy, there's a corn field! ... Look, there's a cow going into the barn! ... There's a farmer ploughing! ... There's a pond with ducks on it!" The father, who was reading his newspaper, wasn't very responsive. He just kept saying: "Uh huh ... uh huh ... uh huh."

Finally, he became annoyed, and a little embarrassed because of all the other passengers who were listening and smiling. He turned to them and said: *"Please don't mind her. She still thinks everything is wonderful."*

Isn't it sad when we lose that; the wonder of childhood? When we are so busy doing those things that we think matter but which don't really matter all that much and we fail to stand still and allow our eyes to be filled with the wonder of the universe, the beauty of nature.

To wonder and to realise that as the hymn puts it: *"All things bright and beautiful, all creatures great and small; all things wise and wonderful. The Lord God made them all. And so often we miss all that."*

We so often lose our sense of wonder at what God has given to us and done for us. It could very well that was one reason why Jesus brought a little child into the midst of his disciples and said: *"Unless you become as a little child you will never experience the Kingdom of God."* For a little child has wonder, a little child has a simple faith.

Here's a thought! Once a week, allow a child to take you for a walk.

TAKE TIME TO TALK

For one fleeting moment our eyes met; but there was no sign of recognition, no hint of a smile, no depth; nothing.

But then I was sitting in the train in the London underground; and that's just what its like there; people sit staring into space, or their ears are wired up tuned into 'Highland Radio '; their nose in a book or sitting gazing lovingly at the object of their desire; their mobile phone.

Willing it to ring; hoping that someone will communicate with them from the outside world.

We are all created for relationships but we live in a world where people don't talk anymore. Our busy lives crowd out the art of conversation and where the only words heard in the home are "Be quiet","I'm watching this" and "Don't bother me now."

So make this day a day in which you will take time to talk to people; bid them the time of day as you meet them in the street, give them one of those smiles that only you can give; take time to talk to the people in your homes, at your work and those who just need to hear a friendly voice.

Take time to talk and also take time to talk to God for he wants to hear from you today and he may not have heard from you for some time. Set aside those few minutes of the day to talk to God for he really is interested in what is concerning you and troubling you and he does have time for you.

Remember it's good to talk and it will make such a difference to that other person and to you.

For one fleeting moment our eyes met; and there was that sign of recognition, that hint of a smile and I knew that I was real and I mattered.

MEET HIM AT THE CORNER

In one of his books Dr Leslie Weatherhead tells the story of how on one occasion the journalist Hugh Redmond was experiencing severe nervous strain, not knowing which way to turn in his life. He was staying at a friend's house before speaking to a large meeting.

His friend said: *"You look tired; would you like to escape all this chatter and rest in a room upstairs?"*

And so he was brought up to a room in which a bright fire was burning, an easy chair was drawn up near it and at his elbow was a little table with an open Bible on it. The Bible was open at Psalm 59 and in the margin opposite verse 10 someone had written an interpretation which enlightened his mind.

In the Bible we read: *"The God of my mercy shall prevent (go before) me."* But the interpretation read: *"My God in His loving kindness shall meet me at every corner."*

All of us have the often difficult road of life to travel along, the corners of life to turn. We are all travelling on it at this very moment and we do not know what lies around the next corner.

Yet at every corner of that road we can be assured that there is God to meet us, to meet us with His loving kindness, at every corner of anxiety, of pain and of sorrow.

"God in His loving kindness shall meet you at every corner."

Believe that and you need not be afraid for then you will know that God is there, waiting to meet you at the corner.

LOVING AND ACCEPTING

George was what many people would call a tramp; he looked rather scruffy in appearance, with his tattered trousers, dirty over sized t-shirtand bare feet. One Sunday morning he was walking past a big, beautiful church in the heart of the city and for some reason decided to go in. The church was full, and the sermon was about to begin. George found no seat, and no one moved to try to make room for him.

And so, having walked all the way to the front without finding a seat, he squatted down on the floor in front of the pulpit. The people were shocked to say the least, but did nothing. Then, the minister noticed the Church's most senior elder slowly making his way down the aisle towards George.

Everyone was saying to themselves, more or less: *"You can't blame him for what he's going to do, or say, to that insolent, irreverent young man! That tramp!"*

It took a while for the old elder walking with his stick to reach George and when he arrived at George's spot and dropped his stick to the floor. Then, with great difficulty, he lowered himself to sit on the floor, next to George, guaranteeing that for the rest of the service George would not sit alone. Everyone was choked up with emotion.

And when the preacher finally gained control, he said: *"What I'm about to preach you may never remember. But what you have just seen, you will never forget."*

Whoever they are, whatever they have done, it is our responsibility in the name of Christ to make everyone we meet and everyone who may decide to come in through the doors of our Churches to feel welcome, accepted and important; because they are all loved by God and valuable to him.

For if we believe that nothing can separate us or anyone else from the love of God; then our lives must be lived practising that both in the Church and out in the world.
As Jesus says: *"Always treat others as you would want them to treat you."* (Matthew 7:12 GNB)

NEW BEGINNINGS

Dear John, I was wondering....No! Dear John, I have been thinking... No! Dear John, I am writing to say...No!

Have you ever started to write a letter and then after a few sentences you realise that what you have written is not what you intend to say and so you crumple up the paper; reach for fresh sheet and have another go? It happens to me when I am preparing a talk or a sermon and then I just have to press the delete key on the computer.

Have you ever wished you could do that with life; press the delete key and start all over again? At certain times we all have wished we could make a new beginning and have a fresh start. We have all made mistakes that we wish now we hadn't made. We have all said things and done things that we are sorry about.

The good news that Jesus came to proclaim is that the opportunity of a new beginning, to make a fresh start on your life is being given to us today; so that we might fulfil the plan and purpose that God undoubtedly has for our lives.

The central message of the Bible is of God's dealings with his unfaithful people and of that offer of new beginnings that He gives to those who come to him in repentance. He is as we read in the 18th Chapter of the Old Testament Book of Jeremiah, the Divine potter who can take our broken and misshapen lives and remould them and remake them into something of value and something of use; into what He first created our lives to be.

On this day, this new day, we have this opportunity for new beginnings. Ralph Waldo Emerson once wrote: "A day is a miniature eternity." In the next 24 hours, you can plot a course that will shape your whole life and destiny. In those 1440 minutes there are blessings to be received; opportunities to be grasped; challenges to be accepted; forgiveness to be offered and love to be shared.

What a difference it could make to our lives and the lives of others if we only reached out and received and accepted from the hand of our gracious God this day of new beginnings and fresh opportunities.

Reach out today and receive it!

THE FUTURE DEPENDS ON YOU

There is a fable about a boy who devised a scheme whereby to deceive a very wise old man. Catching a small bird in a snare, and then holding it concealed but alive in his hand, he would ask the old man: *"Is this bird alive or dead?"* If the wise man said it was alive, the boy would give his hand a quick squeeze and then show the bird dead. If he said dead, the boy would simply open his hand and let the bird fly away. So whatever answer he gave, the wise man would be proved wrong. With the live bird in his hand, the boy came with his question: *"Mr Wise Man is this bird dead or is it alive?"* The old man did not look at the boy's hand. Instead he looked full into the boy's eyes and said quietly: *"My son, it is whatever you want it to be."*

Whatever you want it to be! You and I and every one of us all have in our hands that part of the future bound up by the influence we can have in our homes, with our friends and families and with the people in the community in which we live and those we come into contact with every day.

By our thoughts, the words and actions over which we are in control we are shaping and influencing their tomorrows.

So what will the future hold? What will tomorrow be? Listen! God is saying to each of us this day: *"It is whatever you want it to be."* He has placed the responsibility in our hands to shape the future in a world that is often confused and bewildered.

If you do that you will make a difference to the lives of others by helping them to discover for themselves a personal faith in the One who said: *"I have come that you might have life and have it to the full."* (John 10:10 NIV)

The future is in your hands....

TAKE A BREAK

I was standing in a shop when suddenly I heard it. I hadn't heard it for years: "The Yellow Rose of Texas". And the person in front of me started hoking in his pocket until he got out his mobile phone. I have one of those dreadful mobile phones and I think at least 80% of the population must have one, some have them permanently attached to their ears, and people are connected all the time. A phone goes off in a crowded street and 15 other people look to see if it's theirs.

Is it really that important to be connected every second of the day? People don't even seem to have time to enjoy a meal anymore without the phone going off. Something is terribly wrong. Now I know it is important to be in touch with others but do we have to be connected all the time? For it's also important sometimes to disconnect, that you have some time to get some breathing space in your life. Just a little bit of breathing space.

A little bit of breathing space to talk to your children, to spend time with your wife or your husband and have that time with your friends. And especially a little bit of breathing space to have time for God, what some people would call their quiet time. And you can't do that unless you give yourself a little bit of breathing space.

Jesus understood the need for this. Even while living what was a busy and pressurised lifestyle he recognised that it was essential for him to get away, and just disengage and get some time to be on his own.

And that is why He said to his disciples: *"Come off by yourselves; let's take a break and get a little rest."* (Mark 6:31 The Message)

We all need to take time to do just that.

STEPPING STONES

There is an old fable about a little ant who felt he had been given a raw deal. It seems he had been assigned to carry a piece of straw so long and heavy that he staggered beneath its weight.

To add to his frustration, his progress was brought to an abrupt halt by a large gap in the pathway. Seeing no way of getting across that deep divide, he became discouraged and was ready to give up. Suddenly, he thought of a solution. His backbreaking load could actually be turned into a blessing. He carefully pushed the straw over the crack, crossed over it to the other side, and resumed his journey. He had transformed his heavy burden into a friendly bridge.

That in a sense is the secret of life; to turn frustrations in dreams, failures into triumphs, and stumbling blocks into stepping stones.

Have you ever thought of doing just that, turning stumbling blocks into stepping stones?

That is what God did on the cross; He turned the stumbling block of the cross into the pathway to forgiveness and new beginnings.

To be able to turn stumbling blocks into stepping stones is the secret of a happy and contented life.

And if you really thought about it, you could do that today with some particular problem or difficulty in your life.

And most certainly God could help you do just that if you would just take the time to ask for His help.

SIT WITH THEM

A five-year-old girl developed a brain tumour that was diagnosed as being terminal. One night she was rushed into hospital for intensive surgery. The family sat with their minister during the long hours of the operation. As they sat together, one of the elders of the Church quietly slipped into the waiting room and sat with them. He did not say a word. He just sat with this grieving family in prayerful silence.

After 10 minutes or so, the elder quietly got up and left. No words had been exchanged, but this man had connected with that family in a meaningful way during his brief visit.

The father of the girl would say later that no visit had been as meaningful to his family as the silent visit from this one man waiting with them.

We all know that there is real strength and comfort to be found in a presence. We don't want nor indeed do we have always the strength to face up to all the problems, difficulties and sorrows of life. The disciples discovered that; as they were going through the difficult situations of life Jesus was there with them to help, support and guide. Even after his death and resurrection they were sustained by his promise that He would be with them always; right to the end of time. That promise of Jesus is for all of us.

Isn't that good to know?

There is a little verse which I often refer to from the Book of Ezekiel where the Prophet went to the exiles that lived at Tel Abib near the Kebar River and we read: "*I sat where they sat.*"

That is surely what we all need to do, just to go and sit with someone in those difficult moments of life for it would make such a difference to them. It could well be the most meaningful time you will ever spend in life.

Can you think of anyone who needs your presence just now?

NO FREE LUNCH

You have often heard it said that there no such thing as a free lunch and isn't that true? Free gifts with your petrol but you have got to buy the petrol to get the gift. Buy one get one free but you have got to buy the one and it may be that you only need the one anyway.

We have all received many offers for free goods and services. They come in all shapes and sizes! A letter drops in through the door, you have just won a free gift but you have got to send a substantial amount to cover the package and the postage, which is often more than the actual prize.

Or there is that postcard telling you that you are the winner of a holiday, TV, or car. "Just telephone this number to receive your free prize." The catch is you have to go along to some hotel where someone tries to indoctrinate you into believing that you should buy a time-share property. And people often end up paying out more than they can afford and the prize turns out not to be so "free" after all.

Free offers are everywhere - in the shopping centres, on the street, over the phone, on our computers. I especially love those little free samples of food they hand out in the supermarkets; you can keep going back until you have enough for a "free" lunch.

The truth is there is always a catch. I have never found one yet where there hasn't been a catch. There is no such thing as a *free* lunch. There is always a hidden agenda behind the *free* gift.

But there is one gift that is free. It is the gift that God offers to us through His Son. It is the gift of forgiveness. It is the gift of life in all its fullness to those who put their trust in him. It isn't a gimmick. There is no catch, no hidden agenda. He gave His life freely, to save us. What better gift could there ever be?

And it really is free!! And the really good news is that it is for you!

HIS LOVE NEVER FAILS

A farmer once printed the words GOD IS LOVE on his weather vane. When someone asked the farmer if he meant that God was fickle as the wind; the farmer replied: *"No, I mean that God is love whichever way the wind blows."*

"If the wind blows from the cold north, God is love. If the wind is blowing out of the east, God is love. If the wind blows from the south, God is love. If the wind blows from the west, God is still love."

I think that is a good message for us to remember that no matter what way the wind is blowing or how strong the gale or heavy the rain and we certainly get plenty of that here in Donegal. In spite of it all, God is love. He loves you no matter what. He loves you in good times and in bad times and you can always depend on Him to be there for you in every situation of life.

There are times when you will say to someone: "I'll be thinking about you."

Perhaps you will but maybe you will not.

You will say: "I'll pray for you." Perhaps you will, but maybe you will forget.

For we say such things don't we? But do we always follow up on what we say? We should and we must but we don't, not always.

But God says to you and to me: "I will be with you! I will be there for you always!" And He will; He is there for you today and every day. No matter what, His love will always be there for you.

It is as Paul says: *A love that always protects, always trusts, always hopes, always perseveres.* God's love is a love that will never fail you or let you down. It is such a love revealed to us in the cross of Christ.

Wouldn't it be so good if we could love like that?

DO YOU KNOW WHO YOU ARE?

The story is told of a former Moderator of the Presbyterian Church who was visiting in a residential home. He went up to one elderly lady, shook her by the hand and asked: *"Do you know who I am?"* She replied: *"No, but if you go and ask that lady at the desk she might be able to tell you who you are."* I don't know whether he asked the lady or not or whether she was able to answer his question.

We have all heard similar stories to that of people asking such a question and getting different answers.

Do you know who I am? Do you know who you are? Good questions, those.

Well you know your name, where you come from and lots of other things about yourself. But do you really know who you are and who you are meant to be?

Well the Bible gives us the answer, for it tells us that we are sons and daughters of God and we find our true selves when we accept and realise that. For God gives to us our true identity; He is the one who gives us purpose and meaning in life and the one who has a plan for your life right now.

Do you know who you are? You will do if you repent from your past and turn back to God and allow Him to mould and guide your life. He is the only one who can give your life true meaning and purpose indeed as Jesus promises *"life to the full"*. (John 10:10)

BALANCE IN LIFE

A former chairman of the Coca-Cola Corporation put up the finance for a beautiful golf course and residential complex on the coast of Georgia. He was someone who set a tremendous pace in life, smoked numerous packs of cigarettes a day but sadly before he ever saw the complex completed, he died from cancer.

Shortly before he died he began looking back on his life and didn't seem to like what he saw, because in a speech to some students at university he said: *Imagine life as a game, in which you are juggling some five balls in the air, you name them. Work, Family, Health, Friends, Your spiritual life; and you're keeping all of these balls in the air. You will soon understand that your work is a rubber ball. If you drop it, it will bounce back. But the other four balls, your family, health, friends and your spiritual life are made of glass. If you drop one of these, they will be irrevocably scuffed, marked, nicked, damaged or maybe even shattered. They may never be the same. You must understand that and strive for balance in your life.*

It is necessary for all of us to work hard and to give the best that we can - indeed that is what God expects of us. But it is also necessary to take some rest and also strive for balance in our lives; for a life balanced in every part just like a balanced diet is what we need.

Just think what a difference it would make if you could achieve that balance that would enable you to live each day at God's pace.

What difference might it make to our homes, families, work and our relationship with God?

Jesus said: *"Seek first God's kingdom and his righteousness, and all these things will be given to you as well."* (Matthew 6:33 NIV)

HE NEVER CHANGES

When Lloyd C Douglas, author of The Magnificent Obsession, The Robe and other novels, was a university student, he lived in a guesthouse. Downstairs on the first floor was an elderly, retired music teacher, now infirm and unable to leave the apartment.

Douglas said that every morning they had a ritual they would go through together. He would come down the steps, open the old man's door, and ask, "Well, what's the good news?"

The old man would pick up his tuning fork; tap it on the side of his wheelchair, and say: *"That's middle C! It was middle C yesterday; it will be middle C tomorrow; it will be middle C a thousand years from now. The tenor upstairs sings flat, the piano across the hall is out of tune, but, my friend, that is middle C!"*

The old teacher had discovered one thing upon which he could depend, one certainty in a changing world.

I wonder have you discovered anything like that in your life. You can do if you put your trust in the love of God. For His love never changes; for He loved you yesterday, He loves you today and He will love you tomorrow and on into eternity.

Paul, describing this love of God, says in his letter to the Corinthians: *Love never fails, never gives up, love is eternal.*

The Letter to the Hebrews expresses it: *Jesus Christ is the same yesterday, today and forever. .*

He is the one upon whom you can depend, one constant reality in life and one sure thing in the midst of the confusion of life.

He has promised that *He will be with us always, to the very end of the age.* (Matthew 28:20 NIV)

TWENTY FOUR HOUR SERVICE

You have seen the signs; 24-hour breakdown service; 24-hour onsite service; open 24/7.

Did you ever realise that God gives us just that, 24 hour service. As the Psalmist says: *"He who watches over you will not slumber; indeed, He who watches over Israel will neither slumber nor sleep."* (Psalm 121:3-4 NIV)

The Methodist Bishop, Dr Quayle, told how once when he was burning the midnight oil, he happened to glance at the open Bible on the desk and his eyes fell on those words of the Psalmist: *"He who watches over you will neither slumber nor sleep."* It seemed as if the voice of God was saying to him: *"There is no need for both of us to stay up all night, Quayle, I'm going to stay up anyway. You go to bed and get a good night's sleep."*

You know those nights when you are finding it difficult to sleep because there is something on your mind; some worry, fear, anxiety and doubt. You start thinking about all those things that need to be done the next day or the next week. It may be that you are concerned about what you may have said to someone or you are worried about what the future may hold for your health or the health of a loved one. It could be a number of things and you keep turning them over and over in your mind and you cannot sleep.

Like the Psalmist, why not commit your concerns unto God and leave them there? Knowing that the one who has been with you during the waking hours will be watching over you as you sleep, still working actively on our behalf remembering that His presence is always with us so that we can get a good night's sleep.

So when you go to sleep at night remember those other words of the writer of the 127th Psalm: *"He gives to his beloved sleep."* It is for your benefit so resting in the assurance that He is present with you: *Get a good night's sleep.*

GOOD MORNING

8 7 4

THE JOURNEY TO FAITH

Some years ago I met with a person going through a difficult period in her life; the mist was down, the darkness had descended; feeling that she was in a deep dark tunnel searching for the light.

She found herself to be surrounded by people who said: *"Have faith in God and all will be well."* But how can you have faith when you can't find faith?

She was given books to read that depicted the Christian faith as one nice easy journey but she couldn't see it that way and if the truth were told, it so often isn't that way. For often such books fail to tell the journey it took to reach that point of faith; the moments of doubt, the disbelief, the times we question whether there is a God at all. The lonesome valley we often have to walk through to get to the other side.

I could tell you that I went to Edinburgh recently, how I had a most wonderful time, visited all the historic sights, even had a tour of the new parliament buildings. The hotel I stayed in was great and the food was good and the people lovely. I could tell you all that but I didn't mention the journey, how the boat was late, the weather atrocious, the roads crowded, and road works seemed to be everywhere. And yet it was the journey that got me there.

The journey to find faith is not always the shortest, not always the easiest, for it is often the long and hard road but it is well worth it; for then you will come to put your complete trust in the one who will always be with you through those difficult journeys of life.

It is so often those who seek to find faith and who meet with moments of despair, doubt and disbelief that end up with a stronger faith at the end.

I am so glad that my friend was able to walk through the darkness and find such a faith.

DYING BEFORE YOU LIVE!

The writer Gerald Kennedy recounts the rather startling experience of a man who visited the Bell Laboratories. On the desk of one of the executives he saw a machine that truly represents the end of the line. It was a small wooden casket with a single switch on the side. When you flip the switch there is a buzzing sound, the lid slowly rises so that a hand can emerge. The hand reaches down turns off the switch and goes back into the box. The lid then closes and the buzzing ceases. That's all there is to it; a machine that does nothing but switch itself off.

The sad thing is that that can be like many human lives today; people who awaken each morning with no other purpose than to come home again in the evening and to plump down in the chair, switch on the Television and then fall asleep. The truth is that it could have symbolised my life at one time; one day following the next with little meaning and purpose.

You may remember what I have often thought was a somewhat morbid children's prayer: *"Now I lay me down to sleep, I pray the Lord my soul to keep, if I should die before I wake I pray the Lord my soul to take"*

But is it not true that so many people in our world today die before they really live? Die before they really live because they give up trying; dying before they really live because they can find no meaning and purpose to life or because any purpose they have is one of selfish ambition.

It is into this seemingly, meaningless situation that God comes to us through the words of the Prophet Jeremiah: *"For I know the plans I have for you, says the Lord; plans for good and not for evil, to give you a future and a hope."* (Jeremiah 29:11 NIV) God wants to give you hope and a future in the midst of what may seem a meaningless existence at this moment in your life.

In the midst of the busy routine of life just take a moment to stop today and seek His guidance and His purpose for your life right now.

HAPPINESS IS LIKE A BUTTERFLY

I'll be happy when I get that new car, I'll be happy when I get that bigger house, I'll be happy when I get that pay rise, I'll be happy when I get my holidays. I'll be happy.

We are all on the road in the search for happiness but the trouble is that once we have got what we thought would make us happy we begin to think of something else that will make us even happier.

We want this or that and if we don't get what we want we keep thinking about all that we don't have and we remain dissatisfied.

Instead of thinking about what we don't have, perhaps we should begin to think about all that we have and be at least thankful for that.

Years ago we use to sing the chorus in Sunday School: "*Count your many blessings, count them one by one and it will surprise you what the Lord has done*"

So make a point today to start counting those blessings and start thinking more about what you have than what you want. If you do your life will start appearing much better than before. For perhaps the first time in your life, you'll know what it means to feel satisfied and to be content.

St Paul wrote to the Church at Philippi: "*I have learned to be content whatever the circumstances.*" (Philippians 4:11 NIV)

Not what you want but what you have.

Someone has said that happiness is like a butterfly. When you chase it you never catch it but if you sit quietly one day it will come and light upon your shoulder.

NEVER LOST WHEN!

A little girl was walking with her Father through the centre of a city in which they had just come to live. They turned corner after corner, taking in one sight after the other.

After some time the little girl looked up and asked: *"Daddy are you lost?"* Instead of answering her directly, he tightened his grip on her little hand and smiling warmly asked: *"Why, are you lost?"* *"Oh no!"* she said brightly. *"I am with you Daddy! How could I be lost?"*

In some ways that is a very good parable; for how can you and I be lost as long as we know that our loving God is with us and that we are walking hand and hand with him?

When we are walking with God we are never lost. Even when we are lost, when we wander away from his ways, when we fail to follow his will for our lives, when as the poet Rabbie Burns says: *"We wander in those pathways we know we ought to shun."* Even then we are not completely lost, for God is still out there, still knowing where we are; still looking to bring us home for that is His desire for every one of us.

We can never be lost if we know that God is with us and we are walking hand and hand with Him?

Some of Jesus' last words were: *"Surely I am with you always, to the very end of the age."*

He assures us that He is with us always, today, tomorrow and forever. With our hand in His, we can walk with confidence through each today and all of our tomorrows. And if we listen He will speak to us and speak with us and we will never ever be lost if we listen to His words of guidance and of help.

So reach out today and put your hand into the hand of God and He will lead you through and lead you on.

MAKING IT BETTER!

There is the moving story of what happened at one of the competitions held for those who were disabled, mentally or physically; nine contestants assembled at the starting line for the 100-yard race. At the sound of the starting gun they all started out, as best they could, but with the relish to run the race, to the finish and win.

All, that is, except one boy who stumbled. He tumbled over a couple of times, and began to cry. The other eight heard the boy cry. They slowed down and paused and then every one of them turned around and went back. One girl with Down's Syndrome bent down and kissed the boy and said: *"This will make it better."* Then all nine of them linked arms and walked together to the finish line. Everyone in the stadium stood, and the cheering went on for more than 10 minutes.

Why did they do that? I think it was because they all had the same heart; they were all bound together with love for one another. They knew that the objective was to win, but that the greater objective was to cross the finish and it was better to do it together, than to leave one behind, hurt and crying and alone. As Paul writing to the Christians in Rome said: *"Rejoice with those who rejoice and mourn with those who mourn"* (Romans 12:15 NIV)

That is what Jesus does for us; He comes back to lift us up when we fall, to support us when we stumble and help us to the line. And that is what some of us may need to do for someone we know who is finding life tough at this very moment.

Here is the question for you today. Is there someone you know that you need to go back for, who has been left hurt, crying and alone?

In his parable of the Last Judgement Jesus said: *"If you did it for one of the least of these my children, you did it for me."* (Matthew 25:40)

WHY DON'T YOU DO IT?

A girl brought her fiancé home for dinner. After dinner, the fiancé and the girl's father went into the study for a man-to-man talk.

"So, what are you doing right now?" asks the father. *"I am a theology student,"* replies the fiancé.

"Do you have any plans of employment?" *"I will study and God will provide."*

"What about the children?" asks the girl's father. *"God will provide."*

"And your house and car?" *" God will provide,"* says the young man.

After the chat, the girl's mother asked the father: *"So what did you two talk about?"* Her husband replied: *"He has no plans for employment, but on the other hand, he thinks I'm God."*

That young man had got it partly right; for it is true that God does provide for us but at times He also asks us to play our part in that provision.

There was Moses standing crying unto God at the Red Sea and God says: *"What are you crying unto me for? Tell the children of Israel to move forward".*

So often God's answer to our prayers is simply to tell us to go and do it ourselves.

You want peace? Well then go and do something to make that peace. You want the hungry fed? Well go and do something to feed those who are hungry.

In the book of Ezekiel we find the prophet lying prostrate on the ground his face in the dust and God says to him: *"Son of man stand upon your feet and I will speak with you"*. But first he had to stand, he had to make the effort and when he did that he found that God was with him.

What is it that you want? What is it that you are asking God for? Listen and you might well hear God saying: *Begin by doing something about it yourself and then you will find that I am with you; that I indeed will provide.*

GREY HAIRS

A man entered a restaurant and asked the waiter for a glass of water. "Certainly Sir," said the waiter and brought it to him. Immediately the man took it and threw it into the waiter's face. Quickly grabbing a napkin, he helped the waiter dry his face while he apologised with great regret.

"I'm so sorry," he said. *"I have this compulsion to do this. I fight it, but I don't know what to do about it." "You had better do something about your problem,"* the waiter replied. *"You can be sure I'll remember you and will never serve you again until you get help."*

It was months before the man entered the restaurant again. When he asked for a glass of water, the waiter refused. Then the man explained that he had been seeing a psychiatrist and that his problem was solved.

Convinced it was now OK to serve him, the waiter brought in the water. The man took the glass and splashed the water into the waiter's astonished face. *"I thought you were cured,"* the shocked waiter screamed. *"I am,"* said the man. *"I still do it, but I don't feel guilty about it anymore."*

Sadly that can be true of your life and my life; we do things that once made us feel so guilty; but we keep on doing them and somehow we don't feel guilty anymore.

We have allowed our standards to slip; we have somehow managed to blot out the voice of conscience.

Meditate on these words of the prophet Hosea: *"Grey hairs were here and there upon them and they knew it not."* (Hosea 7:9 AV) We do not always notice the first grey hair but then there is another one and another one.....

Remember these words of Paul in his letter to the Christians in Rome: *"Do not be conformed by the standards of this world but let God transform you inwardly by a complete change of your mind".* (Romans 12:2 GNB)

STRAPPED TO THE TRAILER

Some people who had just got themselves a boat for the first time were having somewhat of a problem. They had just got their boat into the water but no matter how hard they tried, they couldn't get it going properly. It was very sluggish no matter how much power was applied.

After about an hour of trying to make it go, they managed to *putt putt putt* to the quayside, hoping someone there could tell them what was wrong. A thorough top side check revealed everything in perfect working condition. The engine ran fine, the outboard drive went up and down, and the propeller was set at the right pitch.

Then one of the men who had been trying to help jumped in the water to check underneath. He came up choking on water, he was laughing so hard. Under the boat, still strapped securely in place, was the trailer. Now remember, this is a true story.

Sometimes we go through life like that. In the letter to the Hebrews we read these words: *"Let us throw off everything that hinders...and run with perseverance the race marked out for us"*. And Paul writing to the Church at Philippi says: *"One thing I do, forgetting what is behind, I stretch towards what is ahead to win the prize for which God has called me heavenward in Christ Jesus."*

To leave the past behind, we won't always be able to forget it, nor should we at times. You can't forget a loved one who has died, or when a tragic accident has taken away someone so dearly loved.

But you still have to go on; you can't remain there strapped to the trailer of your hurts or your failures; your sorrows or your disappointments. You can't keep on putt, putt, putting through the rest of your life.

So whatever may be holding you back today maybe it's time to let it go - and get on with the rest of your life.

TIME TO DECIDE

A man who had retired from his profession thought that he would like to work on a farm. He got a job on a local farm and the farmer got him to clean out the byre, whitewash some of the farm buildings and then the farmer was going away for the day and he wanted to give him a job that would occupy him the whole day. So he took him into the barn and asked him to sort out the potatoes into large, medium and small and to set aside a particular size for seed.

When the farmer came home in the evening; he went to the barn, and found the man walking up and down the barn wringing his hands, almost in tears. *"What's the matter?"* the farmer asked. Well he answered: *"I don't mind cleaning out the byre or painting the buildings but for pity's sake, don't ask me to make a decision."*

Now that story can be true about many people today, many people who are unwilling or who just can't make a decision.

But there are certain things in life that we must decide and which ought to be a matter of decision. There are times in life when we must simply decide.

And as you read this you may be someone who needs to make a decision today; about seeing about that problem with your health, a decision about the family, about work, a decision about something that has been keeping you awake at night; and more importantly a decision about your relationship with God.

Whatever it is you do have to decide. So determine to make that decision today.

Joshua said: *"Choose for yourselves this day whom you will serve. But as for me and my household, we will serve the Lord."* (Joshua 24:15 NIV)

It may be time for you to make that decision in your life!

LET THE CAT EAT THE HERRINGS

I haven't had a herring for years; I used to have then at least once a week when a man came round the countryside selling them. I must say they were very nice although the bones were at times hard to deal with.

Some years ago there was a play on television where a family was having herrings for tea but the daughter wouldn't eat hers. The father insisted that she did and that she wouldn't get anything else to eat until she ate the herrings. So every meal time for the next couple of days the herrings were set down in front of her but she still refused. The problem was solved when the cat got into the kitchen and ate the herrings.

It is so true that it can often be the trivial and unimportant things that can cause division within families and between friends; things that in the whole scheme of life do not matter all that much.

It may be that you are experiencing such division from someone at this moment in your life. Some grievance from the past is still holding you back from becoming close again as a family; a resentment about a word spoken that wasn't really meant as you took it to mean; and you are cut off from your parents, your son or daughter or someone who use to be such a good friend.

Maybe the time has come to get yourself a cat that will eat those herrings and those red herrings in your life.

And make this the day when you will decide to forgive others as you would want them to forgive you for remember the day will come if it hasn't already come that you too will need to be forgiven and we all need to be forgiven by God.

For if you forgive those who sin against you, your heavenly Father will also forgive you. (Matthew 6:14)

LISTENING TO THE NEWS

I waken up every morning to the radio and as I listen to the news it often doesn't give much reason for hope. Indeed when we listen to the news of all that is happening in our world and indeed even in our own land we can begin to despair and to wonder what the future holds for us as a society or indeed if there will be any real future at all.

For hardly a day goes past when there is not another killing; mugging or someone is killed on our roads. We are so overwhelmed by the evil that seems to surround us in society and wonder if things can change and if there is any hope. It would be so very easy for to lose heart and just give in to despair, as indeed many people have in our society.

Then we come to Easter and we are reminded again to the cross and resurrection. Reminding us the God in Christ has won the victory over sin, death, violence and despair and that there indeed can be a tomorrow for everyone of us. A tomorrow that it is full of hope and full of promise and full of assurance because Christ is alive and his presence is always with us.

And all we need to do is to step out with God into that new tomorrow to defy the odds that can often be seen to be stacking up against us. Knowing that as Paul says in his letter to the Romans that: "*Nothing, nothing that this world can throw at us, nothing not even death can separate us from his love. Our fears for today, our worries about tomorrow, and even the powers of hell can't keep God's love away. Whether we are high above the sky or in the deepest ocean, nothing in all creation will ever be able to separate us from the love of God that is revealed in Christ Jesus our Lord.*" (Romans 8:38-39)

"*How sweet to hold a new born baby, and feel the pride and joy he gives; but greater still the calm assurance. This child can face uncertain days because He lives.*"

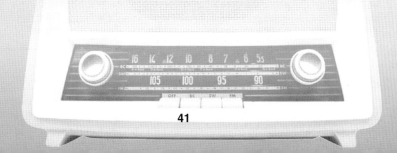

A CHANGE FOR THE BETTER

One man was convinced that the most beautiful word in the English language was WHICH. When his friends questioned him, he said this:

I was afflicted by alcoholism. All my money went into the bar. Every Saturday, I drank until I had nothing left, and then I rolled home and flung the remaining few pounds in my wife's lap. Through all the years I was a slave to drink, I never had any really good clothes. I hated myself and most decent people despised me. Then I met God and was gloriously changed...I cut the drink out entirely. I dropped the filthy talk and gave my wife her proper week's money and began to buy little extras for the home. As the months went by, I even began to get together some new clothes.

One autumn evening, six months after this change came over me, I said to my wife: "Let's go out for a walk." She went upstairs to put her hat and coat on and while she was there I called out: "Bring my overcoat down with you." And do you know what she said? She said, "WHICH?" WHICH! I couldn't answer for a moment. I was staggered by the word WHICH. I actually had TWO.

Here was a man who for so many years had wasted so much of his life and his money now he had two overcoats. Now by the grace of God he was changed and because of that his circumstances changed as well.

Maybe he was the same man who having had a problem with alcohol became a Christian and his workmates began to mock him. *"Surely,"* they asked: *"you can't believe all those miracles. You don't believe Jesus turned water into wine."* The man replied: *"I don't know whether he turned water into wine but I do know that in our house he has turned beer into furniture."*

Paul, writing to the Church in Corinth, said: *"Anyone united with Christ gets a fresh start, is created anew. The old life is gone, the new life begins."* (2 Corinthians 5:17)

God offers to each one of us the opportunity of a new beginning and it can begin right now for someone who is reading this today.

DECIDING AND DOING

There is the old riddle about five frogs sitting on a log. They all decided to jump off. How many were left? Well the answer could be one but it could really be any number up to five because there's a big difference between deciding to do something and actually doing it.

All of us at some time or other have had those decisions we have made but never carried through; those good intentions we had which came to nothing.

When you decided to apply for that job, when you decided to visit that friend you hadn't seen for a long time; when you decided to tell someone your true feelings. Things that you decided or intended to do but things you never did.

The trouble is that there is always so much against us carrying through our decisions; all those other things that call us away; that crowd in upon us, the rush of a busy life; the fear of what people might say; all those things that catch our attention that cause us to forget the intention.

So if you have decided to do! Why don't you carry the decision through this week?

If you have decided to visit that friend whom you haven't seen for a long time or write that letter, why don't you?

If you have decided to spend more time with your family, why don't you?

If you have decided to walk more closely with God, why don't you? For that could be the greatest decision that you will ever make and it will make those other decisions so much easier.

The difference is in the deciding and the doing. The difference is in deciding to jump off the log and actually jumping off the log. Perhaps you need to take that jump in your life this week.

"Now is the time!" said Jesus, *"Now is the day of salvation!"* Not tomorrow, not next week, or the week after but now is the time to carry out that decision you have been holding back from for so long before it may be too late.

Did you hear that old John is dead; John dead? Why I saw him only yesterday and I intended to....!

GOD IS STILL GOD

Gladys Aylward, who was often known as the little woman, was a missionary to China more than 50 years ago. You may have seen the film "The Inn of the Sixth Happiness" starring Ingrid Bergman which told the story of Gladys Aylward's life. When the Japanese Army invaded China she was forced to flee but she could not leave behind the people she worked with. With only one assistant, she led more than 100 orphans over the mountains to freedom.

During her harrowing journey out of war-torn Yangchen, she grappled with despair as never before. After a sleepless night, she faced the morning with no hope of reaching safety. A 13-year-old girl reminded her of their much-loved story of Moses and the Israelites crossing the Red Sea.

"But I am not Moses," Gladys cried in desperation.

"Of course you aren't," said the girl. *"But God is still God!"*

And on those words Gladys Aylward rested her faith, and eventually made it to free China with all one hundred orphans. Gladys and the orphans made it through. God was with them on the journey, and waiting for them at the end.

And this is true of whatever we face in life. We may not be sure of where we will end up in life, but God is there ahead of us waiting for us, just as God is with us on the journey. He is the God of the past, the present and the future.

When going through the anguish of a broken relationship, when facing up to sorrow, when making those difficult decisions, when going through financial crises, in the midst of a terrible situation, when struggling with health, God is with us, and on the other side of the pain and the hurt and the despair and the disappointment, God is there waiting for us.

Just remember when facing those problems of life that God is still God.

BRING YOUR UMBRELLA

It hadn't rained for weeks, the fields were brown from lack of water, and the crops lay wilting. The people got up every morning and looked to the sky in hope that there may a sight of a cloud.

Things were so bad that the local clergy called for an hour of prayer in the town square the following Saturday. They asked that everyone brought an object of faith for inspiration.

On the Saturday everyone turned up for this time of prayer, filling the square with anxious faces and hopeful hearts. There were a variety of objects clutched in the hands of the people, bibles and hymn books, prayer books and rosary beads

When the hour of prayer had ended, as if on command, a soft rain began to fall and a cheer went up from every corner of that square as they held the objects they had brought in gratitude and praise.

But from the middle of the crowd one symbol of faith seemed to outdo all the others. A small nine-year-old child had brought an umbrella.

Didn't Jesus once say: *"Unless you become as a little child you will never enter the kingdom of heaven."* For you see; a little child has trust, a little child has a simple faith.

And Jesus also said: *"Ask and it will be given to you; seek and you will find; knock and the door will be opened to you. For everyone who asks receives; he who seeks finds; and to him who knocks, the door will be opened."* (Luke 11:9 NIV)

Do you believe that? Really believe it? If you do will you bring your umbrella?

St Augustine once said: *"Faith is to believe what we do not see and the reward of faith is to see what we believe".*

THE WRONG WAY

A woman's husband commuted back and forward to work on the motorway everyday. One day she was listening to the radio and heard about somebody driving the wrong way down the motorway. She picked up the phone, called her husband on the mobile and said: *"Be careful dear there is someone driving down the motorway the wrong way."* And he replied: *"It's worse than that dear, there are hundreds of them.*

Do you ever get like that at times? Life becomes so hectic you don't know which direction you are travelling; there always seems to be that mad rush about life. And when you are rushing in one direction there always seem to be others rushing in the other and sometimes you may even meet yourself coming back.

Because of what has been called the rat race you find it very difficult to slow down; for the trend in life today set so often by modern advertising seems to suggest that the whole secret of happiness in life is to get as much as you can, as soon as you ever can.

And because of this mad race to be what others say you ought to be so many people end up on the scrap heap at an early age because they just can't take anymore, they are burnt out; they have spent themselves completely

But what is the answer? Well the secret is to slow down and just enjoy those moments of solitude; those quiet moments when you can recharge the battery.

That is why when surrounded by the pressures of life Jesus always found the time to go off to some solitary place to get some rest, to take time for himself and time to pray to His father in heaven.

Someone reading this today needs to do just that otherwise you will find yourself heading up the motorway of life in the wrong direction towards disaster.

Slow down and allow God to set the pace for your life before it is too late.

BE A CHRISTMAS FANATIC

It's over for another year – Christmas, that is. You will soon be taking down the decorations, and the cards and all the other trappings of Christmas, putting them in the box and storing them away until Christmas comes round again next year.

But wait! Before you start packing everything away just take care that you don't pack away one very important thing. It is something that would be very useful in your life and in the lives of your friends and family and indeed in our society. What is that, you ask?

The Christmas spirit! Be careful that you don't pack away the Christmas spirit of love, peace and goodwill to all people because we often do just that. We are nice for a season but when the season goes we turn back to our old ways and we forget about the people that we should remember through the year. We fail to share the love that many need to experience in our world.

In one of the Peanuts cartoon, Lucy says to Charlie Brown: *"Charlie Brown, it's the Christmas season. I think we ought to bury our differences, forgive each other and try to be kind and get along."* Charlie Brown says: *"Great! But why just for this season? Why not all year?"* And Lucy says: *"What do you think I am, some kind of fanatic?"*

Wouldn't it be great and what a difference it would make in all our relationships and our dealings with people if we, you and I, would become that kind of fanatic?

So don't pack it away the Christmas spirit with all the other trappings of Christmas, keep it close to you the whole year through. Be a fanatic!

Remember God's love reaches down to us not only on Christmas day but every minute of every day throughout the year. Let us determine to share that love with one another each and every day.

WHAT'S IN YOUR BAG?

It was a film, just a short film that I saw a few weeks ago on a website. A young woman was walking along carrying a black bin bag that seemed to be burdening her down; immediately you began to wonder what was in the bag, a few clothes, maybe she was moving or maybe she was taking some things to the launderette or to the dump. But as she went along the bag seemed to be getting heavier for her and she sat down on a park bench.

As she sat there an older man went past; he was carrying a bag over his shoulders; then there were others, a well dressed man, a woman dressed as a nurse, a young boy, a little girl and they were all carrying their black plastic bin bags. Some seemed heavier than others.

As the girl sat there on the bench a young man came and sat beside her and told her to bring her bag to him that night and he would get rid of it for her. Then you began to realise what was in her bag, and in the bags of the other people; all those things from the past that was weighing them down, the hurts and the grievances, the disappointments and the fears, the sins and failures, the guilt and shame.

The film ends with all the people heading off with their bags towards one point; towards that one man. And as they return they are carrying no bags and they are walking straight and tall and life seems so much easier for them

When I saw that short film I was reminded of the words of a song: *"Take your burdens to the Lord and leave them there; take your bin bag filled with all those things that are weighing you down in life to him."*

The question that every one of us needs to answer today is this: What's in your bag? What are those things that your bag is full off at this moment?

Regret, worry, and hurt, a grievance from the past, disappointment, sorrow, failure. Whatever it is in your bag the time has come to lay them down.

Jesus is saying to someone who is reading this today: *"Are you tired? Worn out? Burned out? Burdened down? Come to me. Get away with me and you'll recover your life. Keep company with me and you'll learn to live freely and lightly."* (Matthew 11:28)

The secret is in keeping company with Him.

AFTER KATRINA

The news headlines have in graphic details spelled out for us the aftermath of the hurricane Katrina which created such a catastrophic situation in Louisiana, Mississippi and the neighbouring states. Indeed a horrific experience for those caught up in such a violent force of nature but nothing compared to what followed, the looting, the violence, rape and murder. In New Orleans we were witnessed the total depravity of humanity and in the middle of it all there were people like you and me who were terrified, hungry, thirsty, and lonely and many cut off from family and friends, living in atrocious conditions.

What we have observed over these past days reminds us that despite all our efforts to make the world a better place, sin and evil and hurt and pain, and complete indifference to the needs of others are still with us. In such a situation many ask: Where is God in all of this? Has God deserted us? I think the answer is that not that God has deserted us but that so many have deserted God and have allowed the spirit of evil to control their living and their thinking.

Where is God then? Well Studdart Kennedy, the famous Chaplain of the First World War, known as Woodbine Willie had such a problem of how to reconcile the love of God with the sordidness, horror and pain of war but when he looked at the figure of Christ on the Cross he came to the conclusion that God is not the one who causes suffering but the one who shares it, as he expresses it in words from one of his poems: *"Well what if he came to the earth today, came walking about this trench; how his heart would bleed for the sights he see'd, aye the mud and the blood and the stench."*

The cross of Christ shows us that God is not the one who causes pain, evil, suffering and disaster but he who enters into it with us. That God does not stand as a mere observer to all that is going on in the disaster area but he is there sharing in the sufferings of the people and he is calling on us too not to be mere observers but to do whatever can to help in such situations. We see God not in the violent erupting forces of nature or in depraved humanity but in the lives of those who are still out searching to bring help and comfort to those caught up in the horror of it all.

And what we all need to know that even in the darkest moments, God is there and there is no such thing as a hopeless situation.

CRUISE CONTROL

In this country we are now able to buy cars with what is called "cruise control". Cruise control is where you set the car to the speed at which you want to go, and then you take your foot of the accelerator and cruise along at that constant speed. Very useful on long straight roads like a motorway but perhaps not so useful on most of the roads we experience here in Donegal.

But there is the story which happened some years ago of a newly retired couple in America who purchased one of the best motor homes they could find. It had cruise control. As they were travelling across the country, the husband got tired and asked his wife to drive while he took a nap. While she was driving she put the camper on cruise control and it worked perfectly. So, after an hour of straight motorway driving she got up to make a cup of tea.

After the accident, she told the Highway Patrol she thought cruise control was the same as automatic pilot. The motor home was a wreck, but thankfully neither of them or no one else was hurt.

But unfortunately, that's not always the case when we try to live our lives on cruise control. When we just keep on going without paying too much attention to what is going on around us and waken up to find ourselves lost and somewhat bewildered.

There are those times when we must be completely in control of our lives and our actions for God calls us to be responsible for how we live our lives.

It could be that you have been drifting on aimlessly through life in a sort of cruise control approach. If you have been doing just that before it could be too late begin to take control of your life today and ask God to help you.

I FANCY YOU!

Some years ago I was sitting in Edinburgh having a cup of coffee when Martha sidled up to me; gave me a wee wink and said: "*I fancy you, Jimmy!*"

Now I hasten to add I had never seen the lady before in my life; she was quite a few years older than I was and to put it kindly, just a little drunk.

And as much as I would like to think that I have got that extra something; those dashing good looks, attractive personality, brilliant repartee I would have to admit that Martha was looking at me through distorted vision. Vision distorted by her loneliness, her lack of friends, the despair that she must have felt within herself as she wandered the streets at night and wandered back to sit alone in her little room with only the glow of the fire to bring some light into her dull, drab, meaningless existence.

Eyes distorted by the alcohol she had taken to shut out the realities of the outside world and how she really felt.

We do that ourselves at times; look at life through distorted vision. Sometimes because of worry and anxiety or because of sorrow, sadness, bereavement, and it's hard to know how we'll ever face up to life in the future. Sometimes because of prejudice, fear, intolerance that makes us think that we are the only ones who know and understand and have the truth.

Or like Martha because of loneliness and its difficult to see the warmth and the caring of the world outside; to see anything that makes life meaningful and worth living.

Indeed we often look at ourselves through distorted vision and I'll leave you to think about that.

But the question I want to leave you with today is this. How do we look at people like Martha? Do we look at them through critical, self-righteous eyes or through the eyes of Jesus?

As we go around this day and in the days to come let us see others as Jesus sees them. Then we would recognise them as people of value, to be loved, accepted, cared for and helped.

For Jesus said: "*Whatever you did for one of the least of these you did for me.*"

A NEW VALUE

It was Christmas time and their mother was talking to the shop keeper and so the two little boys used the opportunity to change the price tags around to what they thought the things were worth; to the bewilderment of the customers and the consternation of the shop keeper.

It has been said that Jesus came into the world like those two boys in the toyshop; setting a new value on everything; seeing with clear eyes and judging by new standards; calling upon people to repent and become like little children; that we should learn to look about us with wonder and see things in their right light; the things that we have taken for granted, the things that we have never really looked at.

The upright, praying Pharisee is made to look ridiculous, the sinful tax collector goes home justified. The son who brings disgrace to the family name is nearer to the father than the faithful, stay at home, hard working brother.

And in the Sermon on the Mount, He presents us with what has been called the "Upside Down Kingdom"; He turns the present values of the world upside down.

Those who mourn, those who are poor, those who hunger and thirst after righteousness, those who are persecuted are blessed while the meek shall inherit the earth.

Changing the price tickets to bring about a little devaluation and revaluation; standing the existing society on its head; turning the world upside down.

Would it not be good if we could do just that with the value we put on things and with the values we put on people?

To look at people not through our own blinkered eyes of intolerance and prejudice but through the eyes of Christ.

For that is what happened on that first Christmas, God sent His son and put a new value on us; valuing us as people who matter to Him.

THERE IF YOU HAD WANTED

There is the story of the man who took his wife for a holiday to Paris. One day he took her into a restaurant for dinner. There were a great many French dishes. When they got the bill, it amounted to £30. The man looked at it and said: *"I'm not paying that; there I am charged for a dish we never touched."* *"Well!"* said the waiter: *"that's your fault, it was there if you wanted it."* Again he said: *"I'm not paying!"* So the waiter brought the manager, and he went over the same ground. *"Three pounds for dish we never touched."* *"Well!"* said the manager: *"that's your fault, it was there if you wanted it."*

"All right," said the man, as he got out his wallet and gave him £25. *"This is £5 short!"* the manager said. *"I know that,"* said the man: *"But I'm keeping that back from you for kissing my wife."* *"Oh, but I never kissed your wife."* *"Oh I know, I know that, but she was there if you had wanted to."*

"There if you had wanted!" As you read through the gospel stories, you so often find Jesus there when people wanted him; there for that blind man who cried out to him outside Jericho; there for the woman who reached out to touch him, there for the centurion whose servant was ill, there for Jairus and his little daughter,

And the good news is and we all want to hear the good news. Jesus is still here today for you and for me and he asks us the same question that he asked the blind man on the Jericho road: *"What do you want me to do for you?"*

David Kossoff, whose son died through drug abuse, wrote a little book of prayers called "Have you a minute Lord?"

Have you a minute Lord? it's about my son, my daughter; it's about a problem at work; it's about something I can't forgive, it's about my health, it's about the pressures of life...it's about?

Well you know, don't you? What it's about.

Have you a minute Lord? He has because He is here, here for you today if you want Him to.

Wouldn't it be sad, tragic even; if you missed out because you just didn't ask?

THE FATHER'S EYES

The singer song-writer Amy Grant in her song My Father's Eyes has the words:

When people look inside my life, I want to hear them say:

> *She's got her father's eyes,*
> *Her father's eyes;*
> *Eyes that find the good in things,*
> *When good is not around;*
> *Eyes that find the source of help,*
> *When help just can't be found;*
> *Eyes full of compassion,*
> *Seeing every pain;*
> *Knowing what you're going through*
> *And feeling it the same.*

I have often said that the eyes are the window to a person's soul. I can tell a lot by looking into a person's eyes; not that I spend my time going round looking into people's eyes. But eyes can tell you a lot about a person; they can reveal a lot about how the other person is feeling.

For even though the face may be smiling when you look into a person's eyes you can see sorrow, perhaps, doubt, joy, fear, anxiety or a sense of insecurity, a feeling of inadequacy or on the other hand you can see hope and joy and love.

The Russian musician Valery Gergiev said: "*It's the eyes that are important. You must make every player in the orchestra see your eyes. They tell them what to do.*"

What about your eyes?

What do other people see when they look into your eyes?

Jesus shows us the love, the compassion, the concern and the empathy in the Father's eyes...

Do you have the Father's eyes, eyes filled with compassion, concern and love?

THE PRESENT MOMENT

In the Sermon on the Mount Jesus gives some words of advice to us: *"Do not worry about tomorrow, for tomorrow will worry about itself."*

If we live for tomorrow our focus will always be on it and we will not be able to enjoy what the present moment has on offer for us. And what Jesus is saying is that we cannot afford to lose today by thinking about tomorrow.

One journalist seeking to highlight the need to live fully **now** tells how her brother-in-law opened the bottom drawer of her sister's chest of drawers and lifted out a tissue-wrapped package. He opened up the tissue and handed her a blouse. The price tag was still attached. *"Jan bought this the first time we went to New York, at least eight or nine years ago. She never wore it. She was saving it for a special occasion. Well, I guess this is the occasion."* She writes, he took the blouse from me and put it on the bed with the other clothes we were taking to the undertakers. His hands lingered on the soft material for a moment, and then he slammed the drawer shut and turned to me. *"Don't ever save anything for a special occasion. Every day you are alive is a special occasion."*

This moment, this day is a special occasion, a moment you can spend with yourself, with your family, with God. Just grasp the present moment.

How many of us, caught up in the hurry of life, in providing for tomorrow, are losing experiences today that will be gone forever? How long does a two-year-old stay two? For how long will your daughter want to be read a bedtime story? How many days in the year do you have that special anniversary? Did you hear that John is dead? Dead! Why I saw him only yesterday and I meant to....

And remember this, for this is of eternal importance; we have only one lifetime in which to get to know Jesus and to commit our lives to him.

So just grasp that moment to be with Him in that quiet place; set aside each day a time for prayer in which you can offload life's stresses to God and leave them there. Set aside time to be with family and friends. Take control of your life and grasp and enjoy the present moment.

The Psalmist says: *"This is the day the Lord has made; let us rejoice and be glad in it."*

HOW CAN WE COPE?

It was on a Thursday evening that I stood at the window looking over Dunfanaghy and you could sense the silence and the sadness. It was a community in mourning at the loss of two young men so tragically killed on the road that morning close to Creeslough; two lives so full of vitality and so full of hope for the future. And the thoughts and the prayers of the whole community were with their parents, families and friends and we must continue to support them in the days and weeks and years to come. The news of what happened must have opened old wounds in the lives of many in our society who in the past have experienced such tragedy in their lives for it is something that is happening all too often in our society.

It is difficult for us to understand how anyone can cope with such tragedy; for tragedy it is; and it is at such a time that we can only be driven back to the words of the disciple Peter when he said to Jesus: *"Lord to who else can we go; for you alone hold the words to eternal life."*

To whom else indeed than to the One who has revealed His great love for us; who says He will be with us and there for us in every situation of life; the one who reaches out to take our hand in His and lead us through the tragedies of life into the light of His eternal presence.

The Psalmist expressed it like this: *"Even though I walk through that deep dark valley, I will not be afraid for you are with me and will comfort me."*

And what is that deep dark valley in the context of the Psalmist life of a shepherd but the way from one green pasture to the next; from life to life eternal.

Oh we will still sorrow deeply because of the death of a loved one but we know that there is such hope beyond death.

As the words of one of the newer hymns puts it: *"In Christ alone my hope is found. He is my light, my strength, my song."*

DO I MATTER?

The writer of the 8th Psalm wrote the words: *"When I consider your heavens, the work of your fingers, the moon and the stars, which you have set in place, what is man that you are mindful of him, the son of man that you care for him?"*

What he was asking and what we too must ask is; in such a vast universe do I really matter all that much?

An elderly man is walking along the edge of the water and stops occasionally, picks up something, and then tosses it into the ocean. He then walks a few steps more, picks up something, and tosses it into the ocean. A young jogger is running along and has been watching the man. Finally his curiosity gets the better of him and he stops and goes over to the old gentleman and asks: *"Excuse me, what are you doing?"*

The man answers: *"Well, I am saving the life of these star fish. The storm washed them ashore last night, the sun will be up in 30 minutes, and then they will all die. I am throwing them back into the water to save their lives."*

The jogger was a bit astounded. *"Old man,"* he said. *"Don't you know that you have thirty miles of beach ahead of you and that millions of those star fish were washed ashore last night. What possible difference do you think that you are going to make?"* The old man took another step picked up a star fish, and with all his might hurled it into the ocean, then turned to the jogger and said: *"Well, son, I guess I made a difference in that one's life."*

"If I can stop one heart from breaking or cure one pain, or help one fallen robin into his nest again, I shall not live in vain."

To go out into the world and make a difference to someone's life, then you'll matter, you will really matter a great deal. We are called to be difference makers.

So go out today and help to make a difference in someone's life.

LET GO OF IT

If you have ever read the book by Charles Dickens "Great Expectations" you may remember Miss Haversham who as a young woman had been swept of her feet by a rogue. Marriage plans were made, the day set, the dresses bought, the wedding feast prepared. Then at 20 minutes to nine on the morning of the wedding day, the bridegroom's letter arrived cancelling the wedding. Miss Haversham refused to accept the truth, pronouncing a curse on her lover; she tried to make time stand still. All clocks in the house were stopped at 20 minutes to nine. And as the years went on Miss Haversham became an embittered and eccentric old woman in a faded wedding gown; the wedding banquet mouldering upon the table.

Refusing to see that there was anything beyond the darkness; beyond the failure, the sorrow, the betrayal and the dejection.

Sometimes grief is like that having a way of imprisoning us and keeping us that way. And it doesn't necessarily have to be grief over the loss of a loved one.

It can be grief over the loss of a job or a promotion or a pay rise you thought you were going to get. It could even be grief over a decision you made years ago. It might be grief because of the break up of a relationship or the rebellion of a child.

But whatever it is that is causing the grief, it is holding you prisoner. You are not developing into the individual God created you to be.

So let it go! Let it go! So that you can grasp the life that God has planned for you from this moment on. Let it go today!

LEARNING TO COOK

Some weeks ago Jenny Bristow, the television cook and author came to give a cookery demonstration in aid of church funds. I was there, hoping to pick up a few tips.

For the truth is I am not a very good cook though I can do a nice line in burnt toast and my cremated barbecued sausages are famous for miles around. But then we are not all good at everything. There are some things that I can do reasonably well, other things not so well and I am useless at DIY, for every nail I hammer in never seems to go in straight for me.

We are not all good at everything, some can cook, others can't and some just won't. No, we are not all good at everything indeed cannot be good at everything we decide to turn our hands to but isn't that a good thing? For we have all been given different gifts and abilities and the whole secret of life is to do what we can do as best we can.

Paul explained it this way when he wanted to illustrate the Church and the same illustration can be used for the whole of life. The illustration of the body; that some are hands, others feet, others eyes, others ears, some part may seem somewhat unimportant but every part is needed and essential for the health of the whole body no matter how insignificant that part may seem to be. Paul said: *"You are the body of Christ and each one of you is a part of it.* (1 Corinthians 12:27 NIV)

Maybe you can't cook, you are not all that good at DIY but there is something that you can do and it is important for yourself and for society that you do it and do it well.

I know everyone there enjoyed the demonstration but I think I'll just stick to the day job.

DON'T GIVE UP

Sometimes as I move around our society, I despair. I despair of lives that are lost and lives that are broken. I despair for people who have given up on God and the church; for children and young people growing up in situations where they have no experience of a sense of belonging to anything or to anyone. Those whose lives seem to be weighed down with a real feeling of hopelessness and that seem to have no chance of finding any real completeness in life.

One young man said to a minister: "*I spent my entire growing up years just feeling invisible in my family. I just kept looking for ways to say to my parents, 'Hello, I'm here. I'm a little person with a love-starved heart. If you'd just show me that you see me, if you'd just convince me that I matter, then I can relax on my inside and grow up.*"

It never happened to him and he wrestled with it throughout his adult life until he could wrestle with it no more.

It is to people like that young man and indeed to all of us that the Easter message comes, as a paraphrase of Paul's words in 1 Corinthians 6:14 has it: "*The same power that raised Jesus from the dead will also give you life.*"

What Paul is saying here in the context of this passage, is that for every one of us God has on offer to us that same life giving spirit that brought Jesus back from death to life and which can bring us from despair to hope, from incompleteness to completeness. That can indeed enable us to become the individual that God created us to be.

And so whatever your situation, he is saying: "Don't give up, don't give way to despair."

God's resurrection power is available whatever your situation to lift you from despair to hope, from doubt to faith, from death to life eternal. And you can receive that power today by simply asking him and so there is no need to give up or give in to despair.

ARE YOU LISTENING?

It is reputed that President Roosevelt got tired of smiling the expected presidential smile and saying the usual things at all those White House receptions. So one evening he decided to find out whether anybody was really listening to what he was saying. As each person came up to him with extended hand, he flashed that big smile and said: *"I murdered my grandmother this morning."* People would automatically respond with comments such as: *"How lovely!"* or *"Just continue your great work!"* Nobody listened to what he was actually saying, except for one foreign diplomat. When the president said: *"I murdered my grandmother this morning,"* the diplomat responded softly: *"I'm sure she had it coming."*

So often when we are trying to say something nobody is really listening. So let us all make this a day when we listen. A day in which we will make a point of listening to those we meet.

When your husband gets home from work and he has something to tell you; when your wife wants to talk about her day.

And when your children come and want to ask you about something, instead of saying: *"Some other time, I'm busy just now, I'm watching this programme,"* just sit down and listen.

Listen to your child. Listen to that friend. Listen to that neighbour.

And listen to God for He must sometimes feel like no one's really listening. When so often many of our prayers are monologues and not dialogues and we listen very little.

So take time today to listen to others and to listen to God because He has something He wants to share with you.

And when you listen, when you listen away from all the noise and rush of life; like Elijah after the earthquake, wind and fire you too may well hear the gentle whisper of God comforting you, reassuring you and challenging you.

Are you listening?

JUST BE CONTENT

I went through an accident-prone stage in my life; first I cracked two ribs, two weeks later I was attacked by a dog and ended up with a broken wrist, three weeks later I tore ligaments in my leg. There I was with my cracked ribs, broken wrist, torn ligaments. There were so many things I couldn't do....use a fork...turn the pages of newspaper...get to the phone quickly. I was feeling somewhat sorry for myself.

I then for some reason began to think of those who never had the use of their hands; who couldn't hear the phone even if it rang all day; who even they could turn the pages couldn't see to read them. Those who have all the money in the world yet lack the things that money can't buy. I then realised how trivial some of the things that can annoy me really are.

And isn't the real secret of contentment to see the pluses of life as well as the minuses; the things you can do instead of the things you cannot do; the things you have instead of the things you have not

If we would just sit down long enough to take some time to add up the pluses and the minuses of life. Perhaps then we would be able to echo those words of Paul that he wrote to the Church at Philippi: *"I have learned whatever the circumstances to be content."*

But then in that same passage Paul goes on to say: *"Through Him who gives me strength; through Christ!"*

For Jesus is the one who found the secret of contentment; he was misunderstood by members of His own family; yet content...forsaken by His friends; yet content; nowhere to lay His head; yet content.

And there in the garden going through the agony of decision with the cross hanging over Him yet content to leave it all in the hands of God speaking those words: *"Nevertheless not my will but yours be done."*

And then at the end of His earthly life we find the secret of that contentment and that peace of mind.

"Father into Your hands I commit my spirit!" He was content to leave it all to God.

You will never find real contentment in life until you too are able to say: "Nevertheless *not my will but yours be done."* Unless you are able to say: *"Father into your hands I commit my spirit!"*

LITTLE MORE THAN NOTHING

"Tell me the weight of a snowflake." A little bird once asked a wild dove.

"Nothing more than nothing," the dove answered.

"In that case I must tell you a marvellous story," the little bird said..

"I sat on a branch of a fir, close to its trunk, when it began to snow - not heavily, not in a raging blizzard: no, just like in a dream, without a sound and without any violence. Since I did not have anything better to do, I counted the snowflakes settling on the twigs and needles of my branch. Their number was exactly 3,741,952. When the 3,741,953rd dropped on the branch, nothing more than nothing, as you say, the branch broke off."

When the little bird had told that story it flew away.

The dove thought about the story for a while, and finally said to herself. *"Perhaps there is only one person's voice lacking for peace to come to the world."*

Nothing more than nothing! Think of the importance that Jesus placed on little things, one farthing, a cup of cold water, a little child in the midst of his disciples.

Jesus said: *You are the salt of the earth...*you...you and you...that one pinch of salt and what a difference one pinch of salt can make to the recipe of life. What a difference there can be when it is left out.

It may only seem to be very little, nothing more than nothing. But today you could make a difference to the life of one person and perhaps even to the life of our society and our world.

JUMPING TO CONCLUSIONS

The owner of a large warehouse was concerned about his profits and decided to make a call to see how things were going. He saw a young man leaning up against a wall apparently not working. The owner asked the young man: *"How much do you make a week?"* The reply was £200. The owner reached for his wallet, pulled out £200, handed the money to the man and said: *"You can leave. We don't need you around here any more. "* As the young man walked away, the warehouse supervisor arrived and the owner asked: *"How long has that fellow been working for us?"* The supervisor looked at the young man as he drove away and replied: *"He doesn't work for us; he was just making a delivery."* The point of this story is one worth learning in life; *don't jump to conclusions.*

But we do jump to conclusions, about things, about people, about what they are like.

We see someone scruffily dressed and we immediately conjure up all sorts of ideas about them and about what they might be up to. We jump to conclusions about people because of how they are dressed, the length of their hair, the schools they go to, and the car they drive, the company they keep and names they have. We jump to conclusions all the time and how often we reach the wrong one for first impressions can often be wrong.

It happened to Jesus when Nathaniel asked: *"Can any good thing come out of Nazareth?"* He was judged because of where he came from. He's only a village lad and later when Jesus went back to his own home village of Nazareth he was judged again: *Is this not only the carpenter's son?* He was judged and indeed even condemned because of his family background.

But Jesus looks at us in a different way, he doesn't jump to conclusions, he just says Follow me!!

Not many people would have seen pillars of the Church in an impetuous person like Peter, or a pair of argumentative brothers like James and John. But Jesus did.

Not many people would have seen much good in a man like Zacchaeus, but Jesus did.

Jesus sees you as you are and He knows what you can be. Only He can turn the one into the other, when He says follow me and you begin to follow.

ANY CHANGES? NOPE!

In 1990 during the BBC Television series "Trouble Shooter" the flamboyant industrialist Sir John Harvey Jones visited the Morgan Car Company and analysed the business. His conclusions were significantly at odds with the views held by the Morgan family, who said so. Even today, many conversations start with reference to the programme, which has entered British folklore.

Morgans are hand-built traditional sports cars. The employees are skilled craftsmen - no mass production, each one completed by the experts. Because of this method they only produce about 11 cars a week, and if you want one you will have to put your name on the waiting list and be prepared to wait for quite a time. The company was hoping that Harvey-Jones would advise them how to increase production without sacrificing any of their traditional quality.

How long have you lived here on earth?

If during that time there hasn't been any significant change in our attitudes; if we are just the same old people doing the same old things in the same old way, with the same old ambitions. Then it may well be time to ask ourselves the sort of questions John Harvey-Jones would ask us and Jesus certainly asks us.

What have you done with your life up to now?

One day I looked at myself
At the self that Christ can see;
I saw the person I am today
And the one I ought to be.

I saw how little I really pray
How little I really do
I saw the influence of my life
How little of it was true.

I saw the bundle of faults and fears
I ought to lay on the shelf
I had given a little bit to God
But I hadn't given myself.

I came from seeing myself
With my mind made up to be
The sort of person that Christ can use
With a heart that he may always see.

It may be time for you to change

TEMPTED NOT TO FORGIVE

"Father, forgive us, as we have forgiven others." I remember hearing Mother Teresa of Calcutta speaking about those words and she said that before them came the words, *lead us not into temptation.* She then went on to say that the greatest temptation we have is the temptation not to forgive or to try to find reasons why we should not forgive. And there would be temptation enough to do that very thing in our world and in our society so many times; so how good it is to hear people speaking words of forgiveness and love in situation where it must be so very difficult to be forgiving.

The Bible tells us that we experience God's friendship when we are prepared to live by God's standards; the standards of mercy, forgiveness and love which God introduced into the world in Jesus Christ. And how can we live by such standards unless we put away that critical spirit, judgmental tongue and pointing finger which is so completely alien to the mind and heart of Jesus?

Paul wrote these words which I use at every marriage service: *"Be kind and compassionate to one another, forgiving each other, just as in Christ God forgave you."* (Ephesians 4:32 NIV)

There is the story told of Robert Louis Stevenson who conducted family worship every morning in his South Sea Island home. One morning in the middle of the Lord's Prayer he suddenly rose from his knees and left the room. His wife followed him out fearing he was ill. *"Is anything the matter?"* she asked. Stevenson answered: *"I am not fit to pray the Lord's Prayer today."*

Forgive us as we have forgiven others; I wonder have we always been fit to pray those words.

DINNAE SLAM IT

A young mother and her little boy were driving down the street. The little boy asked, "Mammy, why do the idiots only come out when Daddy drives?" Some day that little boy will understand that Daddy's anger says more about Daddy than it does about the quality of drivers on the road.

We have all been guilty of it and we have got to see how senseless so much of it is and to realise the harm that it can do to our relationships. Such an outward show of anger or inner resentment can have a harmful effect on our health. One magazine article entitled "Is Anger Killing You?" reported new evidence about the destructive physical impact that's put on your heart when you harbour hostile, angry thoughts. Your anger could be killing you at this very moment.

Paul gives us some other sound advice when, writing to the Ephesians, he says: "*Do not let the sun go down while you are still angry, and do not give the devil a foothold.*" (Ephesians 4:26 NIV)

Life is short and not one of us knows what the future holds. There is the story of the young man from Scotland who was setting out from home to make his way in the world. As he said goodbye to his mother he received a homely piece of advice: "*Whatever happens laddie keep your temper under control, you will often be disappointed and upset but dinnae slam the door*"

Time is short, love is eternal. What a lesson that is to those who would use violence in our world or to any who would hold even a spark of anger or resentment for one short space of time.

So dinnae slam the door!

REACH OUT

One young person tells how just two days before he was to leave high school, his father died suddenly.

It was just two days before my high school graduation. When he died I found myself in a place I'd never been before. I wanted to hear God speak. I wanted to know what he had to say about this situation; how he was going to get me and my family through this difficult time. So I prayed. And I waited for God to speak.

When the day of the funeral came the church was packed. I sat on the front pew with my mother and two younger sisters. The minister spoke, but I don't remember what he said. I continued to wait for God to say something. Then the service was over. It was the tradition of this church to have the family line up in the vestibule. Everyone would file past us and offer words of condolence and encouragement. Tears were shed, hugs offered, and words were given. I don't remember what anybody said to me in that time. But I continued to wait for God to speak.

Then I saw Kim O'Quinn. She was my age. We were in the youth group together. When she got to me, she didn't say a word. She had tears in her eyes. And she simply hugged me and walked off. But I heard God speak. It dawned on me that just months before, I had attended another funeral; the funeral of Kim O'Quinn's father. In that moment she knew exactly what it meant to be me.

Someone out there is suffering today because of the death of a loved one, because of some dreadful experience in life and you have been there; you understand what they are going through. Reach out to them because a word or a hug from you could mean so much.

CALLING YOUR NAME

There was once an old man who had a little spotted dog. The dog was a mixture of many breeds. He was just a mongrel, but the old man loved him because he was all he had. They were constant companions, going everywhere and doing everything together. Every night the dog slept at the foot of the old man's bed.

Then one day the dog disappeared. He was playing in the yard one moment, and the next thing the old man knew he was gone. He searched everywhere for him, looked on every street, around every corner, and talked to every neighbour, but the dog was nowhere to be found. The old man searched all over the town, calling out the dog's name as he went, listening in vain for his familiar bark. The next day was the same and the one after that ..... For weeks the old man searched till finally his neighbours and friends convinced him that there was no use in looking anymore. Surely the dog is dead, they said: hit by a car, no doubt, and crawled off somewhere to die.

Still the old man would not give up hope. Every night, before bed, he went out to the back and called out the dog's name at the top of his voice. This went on for several months. The neighbours were certain that the old man had lost his mind. And then one night, as the old man was calling his name, the little spotted dog came home. The old man never knew where he had been or what caused him to stay away so long, but he was very glad that he had never stopped calling his name.

Perhaps today you may feel like that lost dog; you have wandered off and you don't know where you are; but all the time God has not forgotten you and all he wants is for you to come back to him.

It may be that you are someone who has wandered off from home and family and you haven't seen them for years; all this time they have never forgotten you; they are still calling out your name.

Today may be the day to return home.....

FOLLOWING THE SIGNS

We were going to Kells in Co Meath some years ago. I had never been there before so I studied the map and worked out the right route. As I got closer to Kells I began to follow at the road signs. And there was a sign pointing off to the left for Kells so I turned down it. As I went further and further down the road the narrower it got until I realised that someone had turned the sign to point in the wrong direction.

You can't always trust the signs on the road for people in this country are in the habit of changing them.

And you can't always trust people for you are not always sure that what you hear is what is right. You can't always believe in a promise for promises are often broken; nor can you believe everything you read in the papers or you hear on the radio or television.

And life itself can be a bit confusing at times and you never can be sure if you are doing the right thing or are making the right decisions.

That is probably why Jesus once said: "*I am the way, the truth and the life*"

And those words are true and you can depend on them to point you in the right direction. So why not today test them out for yourself?

And begin to follow the one who leads you on the right road, who speaks the truth to you and offers you life that is full and abundant.

BUSY! BUSY!

In the Book of Genesis we read how God created the world in six days and He saw that it was very good; then we are told on the seventh day God rested from all his work. *"So God blessed the seventh day and hallowed it, because on it God rested from all his work which he had done in creation."*

There, right at the beginning of creation, we find laid out for us the provision for rest and leisure.

But we don't do that today; we don't take the rest that we all need. We are a busy, busy, busy people. Whether we are young or old, rich or poor, married or single, parent or grandparent, come from Donegal or Tyrone or wherever we are all under stress of one kind or another at work, at home in the daily business of living.

Life becomes so hectic you don't know which direction you are travelling; there always seems to be that mad rush about life. We are busy, busy, busy people; people addicted to busy-ness.

I sometimes wonder how in spite of all the advances in technology that have been introduced, we still live every day pressed for time; so pressed for time that we don't take the time to spend with our families and our friends.

So maybe we should take time to pause from the busy-ness and take time to pray this prayer and then act upon it.

Slow me down, Lord!
Ease the pounding of my heart
By the quieting of my mind.

Teach me the art of taking minute vacations,
Of slowing down to look at a flower,
To chat with a friend, to pat a dog,
To read a few lines from the Good Book.

If God needed to take a Sabbath of rest how much more need we to do so.

IMMANUEL

It was a December afternoon; the parents were all waiting outside the gate of the school to pick up their children after the last day of the Christmas term. As the little ones ran out they were all carrying in their hands "the surprise", the brightly wrapped package on which the class had been working for weeks.

One little boy trying to run, put on his coat, and wave to his parents all at the same time, slipped and fell. The "surprise" flew from his grasp and fell on the hard playground with an obvious sound of pottery breaking.

The child's first reaction was stunned silence. But then he set up an inconsolable howl. His father, thinking to make light of the incident and comfort the boy, patted him on the head and murmured: *"Now that's all right. It really doesn't matter son, it doesn't really matter at all!"*

But the child's mother was somewhat wiser and she dropped on her knees on the playground, swept the boy into her arms and said: *"Oh but it does matter. It matters a great deal."* And she wept with her son.

And that is what God reveals to us of himself in Jesus; He is not the parent who dismisses our lives, as if our troubles or problems do not really matter.

But He is the one who comes down to the earth beside us, picks up our torn, bleeding spirits. And says to us: *"Oh but it does matter, it matters a great deal, it matters eternally."*

He is the one who is called *"Immanuel"*, God with us, sharing in every aspect of our lives!

The Word became flesh and dwelt among us; full of grace and truth.

GOOD MANNERS

I was just about to enter the shop when I saw her coming towards me with the pushchair and so, gentleman as I am (sometimes), I stood back and held the door to let her out; but from her not a word of thanks or even a look; it seemed as if she thought it was her right.

There are also those times when you are standing in the queue and someone jumps in ahead of you. Or that time when you are having a conversation with someone and someone else interrupts uninvited.. One man stopped to hold the door open for the woman coming behind him but instead of expressing appreciation, she was furious. She said: *"You don't have to hold the door open for me just because I'm a woman."* He answered: *"I didn't hold the door open because you're a woman. I held the door open because I'm a gentleman."*

I don't know if the Apostle Paul ever had to stand in a queue and someone had jumped ahead; or if he had held a door for someone and they just walked on without a word. Perhaps he had? Maybe that's why we find those words in 1 Corinthians 13 which I hope you will take time to read for yourself. In it we find Paul saying that *love is patient, kind, does not envy, does not boast, and is not proud* and then those words *love is not ill-mannered.*

JB Phillips translates that verse as reading: *"Love has good manners".* You can't get much plainer than that.

Love has good manners. Think about those words today as you meet with people and work with people and within your own home and act towards others and as you would like them to act towards you and continue to hold the door.

RUB THEM OUT

I knew of a head-master who carried around with him a little notebook and if any member of staff did anything that annoyed him or made him angry he wrote their name down and that name was only stroked out when he got his own back.

In 1 Corinthians 13, which speaks about love and what love should be like, we read: *"Love is not easily angered, it keeps no record of wrongs."*

That headmaster would have needed to have paid attention to those words.

Love keeps no record of wrongs. Let us think about that for a moment. Let me ask you a question. How good is your memory? I am sure we would all admit that the older we get the more our memory begins to fade. And you meet that person in the street that you should know and you just can't put a name to them; or you can't remember where you left your car keys or maybe even where you left your car in the car park. You fail to remember your wife's birthday but for some reason you will remember your own.

Memory begins to fade but sadly enough there is a memory that doesn't fade all that easily, the hurts that have been inflicted on us, and the things others have done against us or said about us. And so many people carry that little notebook around in their head that holds on to those records of wrong.

Let me suggest today that you take out the eraser and begin to rub out those memories; for remember that is what God does for you; not only does He forgive you but He also forgets.

"As far as the east is from the west so far has He removed your transgressions from us." Think about those words and act upon them today.

WHEN IS ENOUGH ENOUGH?

Philip Parham tells the story of a rich industrialist who was disturbed to find a fisherman sitting lazily beside his boat.

"Why aren't you out there fishing?" he asked.

"Because I've caught enough fish for today," said the fisherman.

"Why don't you catch more fish than you need?" The man asked.

What would I do with them? You could earn more money and buy a better boat so you could go deeper and catch more fish. You could purchase nylon nets, catch even more fish, and make more money. Soon you'd have a fleet of boats and be rich like me.

The fisherman asked: *"And then what would I do?"*

"You could sit down and enjoy life," said the industrialist.

"What do you think I'm doing now?" replied the fisherman.

It is worth thinking about that for why do we make such a mad rush of life? When is enough enough?

What is it all for in the end? If we have been so busy making a living that we have failed to make a life with our family and our friends.

As Jesus once asked: *"What good does it do if a person should gain the whole world, and yet loses his soul in the process? Or what can a man give in exchange for his soul?"* (Matthew 16:26)

ONE THING AT A TIME

Confession time: I'm a flicker. I have that remote control in my hand and I flick from one channel to the other. I think it is a condition from which many men suffer. I have even been known to attempt to watch two films on television at the same time by flicking from one to the other.

The other day when I was in the car, I noticed the driver next to me at the traffic lights was on the phone, reading some notes and trying to take a drink at the same time. I have seen others putting on their make up, women that is, fixing their hair in the rear view mirror. Not the most sensible of things to do.

We live in a frenzied society where so often we try to do more than one thing at once.

We all do it, try to watch more than one television programme at once while reading the newspaper, speaking to someone while our mind is somewhere else, or sitting in Church listening to the sermon while thinking of all we have to do in the week to come.

But when we do too many things at once, it's impossible to be properly focused on anything and impossible to do anything really well.

A very worthwhile thing that we all need to do is to block out periods of time when we commit ourselves to doing only one thing at a time.

So whether you are washing dishes, talking on the phone, driving the car, playing a game with your child, watching television, talking to your wife or husband, or reading a newspaper, try to focus only on that one thing.

And you know what? You will feel less under pressure and you will actually begin to enjoy what you are doing and it will be amazing how quickly and efficiently you will get things done.

Remember Jesus once gave good advice, about not being worried about tomorrow, about taking each day at a time and I believe He would go on to add, in relation to our frenzied lifestyle: *Do one thing at a time.*

I hope you are taking his advice while you are driving your car today. It will be a lot safer for you and for others.

A NEW GRANDSON

The phone rang at 5.15 am; it was our daughter Judith to say that she was on the way to the hospital and at 7.16am our new grandchild was born.

I believe the birth of a new baby brings hope for this world. As the Indian poet Tagore says: *"Every child comes with the message that God is not yet discouraged with mankind."*

For every child that is born there waits the gospel message. The message that Jesus was born to bring hope for mankind; the hope of salvation; and hope of life anew and life eternal.

But what can we to say to this child new into the family? That two and two make four, that Donegal is the centre of the universe, that the only team to support is Manchester City, that your grandfather is the greatest man who ever lived?

What we should say to this child and to every child is this. Do you know what you are? You are a miracle. You are unique. In all the years that have gone before there has never been another child like you. You are an individual created and loved by God.

You may become a great writer, a famous musician; one day you might even play for Ireland. You have within yourself the ability to achieve the plan and purpose that God has for your life.

And remember this that whatever you become, whatever you do, you are loved and you are special to us, and special to God.

For isn't that just what that child born in Bethlehem came to tell us?

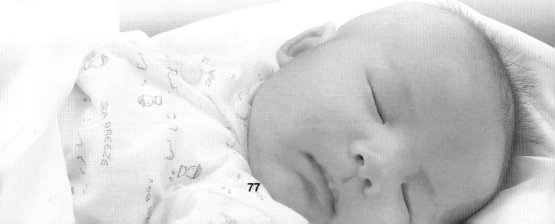

MEMORIES

A man telephoned his friend who was a little bit absent-minded. *"You told me that you went somewhere on holiday last year and it was great place. Where was it?"* he asked. His friend said: *"To tell you the truth I can't remember, give me the name of a flower."* His friend said: *"Chrysanthemum…no it's not that, daffodil, no not that, marigold; that's not it either. It's a shorter word. Rose? Yes that's it. Rose,dear, where was it we went to last year for our holiday?"*

Memory is a wonderful thing, it is something that we are not always all that thankful for until like me, you begin to get that little bit older and you begin to lose it; you can't remember the things that you once remembered.

How important memory is for us and how important it may be for some of you.

Perhaps life is getting on top of you; that relationship is not as good as it once was; the children are becoming a bit of a burden.

It can be helpful today to sit down with your memories; memories of the things that you do have in life that mean so much; of that time when you walked hand and hand and had so much to talk about; memories of how you felt when you both stood before God and made your commitment to one another; memories of the day you looked into the eyes of your newborn baby and the love that you had in your heart; the promises you made.

Just sit down with your memories today and remember the God who loves you and cares for you; and always remembers you whether your own memory be good or bad.

Just sit down with those happy memories and be thankful for them.

FLOWERS OR WEEDS?

A certain king had two servants. To the first he said: *"I want you to travel for six months through my kingdom and bring back a sample of every weed you can find."*

To the second servant the King said: *"I want you to travel for six months through my kingdom and bring back a sample of every flower you can find."*

Six months later, both servants stood before the King. Of the first the King asked: *"Have you carried out my command?"* The first answered: *"I have and I was amazed to find there were so many weeds in the kingdom. In fact, there is nothing but weeds in this kingdom."*

To the king's question the second also answered: *"I have, and I am amazed at how many beautiful flowers there are in the kingdom. In fact there is nothing but beautiful flowers in this kingdom."*

You see it all depends on how you look at things as someone has written: *"Two men looked out of prison bars, one saw mud and the other stars."*

And there was the Apostle Paul cast into prison for years and yet while there in that prison he wrote those words to the Church at Philippi: *"Rejoice in the Lord always. I will say it again: Rejoice! Whatever is true, whatever is noble, whatever is right, whatever is pure, whatever is lovely, whatever is admirable - if anything is excellent or praiseworthy - think about such things."* (Philippians 4)

It all depends on how you look at things and it all depends on how you look on people. If you look for something to criticise you fill find it but if you look at something to praise you will find that too.

You can choose today to look at this world and the people in it through blinkered eyes or you can look through the eyes of God at the world He created and the people He created in his image.

And remember this from a gardening point of view a weed is just any plant growing the wrong place.

Think about that!

Think about it!

EMPTYING THE ASH TRAY

I was driving slowly at a funeral when suddenly I couldn't believe what I was seeing. The driver in the car in front put down his window and emptied the contents of his ashtray out onto the road. There must have been at least 60 cigarette butts with all the accumulated ash. I wondered was that the way he emptied his ashtrays at home - just tip them unto the carpet.

But then I suppose I shouldn't have been all that surprised when you look around and see the mess that we often make of our world. The papers, cans and bottles left behind after a family has had a picnic; the litter around our streets and indeed the chewing gum on the pavements which has become a permanent feature of many towns.

In the book of Genesis we read that God planted a garden in Eden, He put the man He had just made in it to work the ground and keep it in order.

God has given each one of us a responsibility for this world to be stewards of His good creation. We are to tend it and care for it and keep it in order. That surely means that we keep it tidy, we use its resources wisely and in such a way that we will not destroy this world which is our home during our earthly lives.

We have a responsibility towards the environment and those early chapters of Genesis also tell us that we have a responsibility towards other people; that we are indeed our brother's keeper.

Responsible for the environment! Responsible for other people!

Now there's a thought for today and for all the rest of the days as well.

HAPPINESS IS...

I don't know if you have ever written or felt like writing to one of the agony aunts in the magazines. One such letter that was written reads as follows:

"*Happiness is knowing that your parents won't almost kill you if you come home a little late. Happiness is having your own bedroom. Happiness is having parents that trust you. Happiness is getting the telephone call you've been praying for. Happiness is getting good grades and making your parents proud of you. Happiness is being a member of a popular group of friends. Happiness is having parents who don't fight. Happiness is knowing that you're dressed as well as anybody. Happiness is something I don't have.*" Signed, *Fifteen and Unhappy.*

Shortly after the letter was published, "Dear Abby" received a response from a 13-year-old girl who wrote:

Dear Abby: "*Happiness is being able to walk. Happiness is being able to talk. Happiness is being able to see. Happiness is reading a letter from a 15-year-old girl who can do all three things and still says she isn't happy. I can talk, I can see, I can hear, but I can't walk.*" Signed, *Thirteen and Happy.*

What is happiness? And how can we pursue it if we don't know what it is? Remember the song from the musical Oklahoma?

"*Oh what a beautiful morning, oh what a beautiful day, I've got a wonderful feeling, Everything's going my way.*"

Like that 15-year-old girl we tend to regard happiness in that way. When everything's going my way, I'll be happy. But the truth about life is that we can search all our lives but we'll never reach the point where everything's going our way.

So like those two girls it all depends on how you look at things; depends on whether you look at life through positive eyes or negative eyes. It depends whether you look at life through the eyes of the world or through the eyes of God.

As the Psalmist writes happy is the man who trusts in God. So be happy!

NOTHING HE CANNOT DO

At the Sunday School rally some weeks ago we sang the words of the song: *"My God is so big, so strong and so mighty there is nothing that God cannot do."*

There is no way we can cope with the struggles of everyday life all by ourselves, but we don't have to. We have one we can trust to see us through when life becomes difficult. The late Rosalind Russell, noted for her many film portrayals of witty, sophisticated career women, also experienced many triumphs on the Broadway Stage. But perhaps her greatest triumph was her gallant fight against arthritis and cancer. After her death in 1976, this poem was found tucked away in her prayer book:

Trust Him when dark doubts assail thee;
Trust Him when your faith is small,
Trust Him when simply to
Trust Him is the hardest thing of all.

What we all need to remember at times and at especially in those difficult times of life that God is always with us.

One writer put it this way: *"We can risk, because we have a powerful Lord watching over us. We can trust, because we have a forgiving God caring for us. We can step out in faith, because we have a God who is sure to save."*

"Trust Me!" God is saying you today. "Trust Me with your life! Trust me with that problem that you have; that difficulty within the family, with your sorrow. There are storms in life that we all face; there are difficult times; will you trust Him to see you through?"

Indeed as that song goes on to say: *There is nothing that God cannot do.*

MACHINES DON'T ASK

An elderly lady stood in the queue at the Post Office, waiting for stamps when the person next to her said: *"If you only want stamps sure you could get them at the machine."* *"I know,"* she replied, *"but the machine doesn't ask me about my arthritis."*

We all need to know that someone cares about us as people and we all need to care about others. To show an interest in how they are feeling.

Doesn't it mean something when someone knows that you don't take sugar or milk in your tea; that they care enough to have remembered?

And we have a God who cares enough to know everything about us; a God filled with compassion for each one of us.

We live in a world today of hurting people, people are suffering from all kinds of illnesses, physical, mental and spiritual; hurt because of words spoken or a relationship that has broken down.

If you do nothing else today try to be careful with your words for they can make such a difference to the lives of other people.

And if you should do nothing else today ask someone how they really are and be prepared to listen as they tell you.

WATCH WHAT YOU SAY

"Sticks and stones may break my bones, but words can never hurt me" goes the saying but it isn't true. Words do hurt. You know that if you've ever had a parent scold and criticise you, a friend talk behind your back about you, a fiancé break an engagement, the telephone to tell you about the death of a loved one or a doctor give you a diagnosis of cancer. Words CAN hurt. They can be devastating.

A broken bone heals faster than a broken spirit. The Bible says: "Kind words bring life but cruel words crush your spirit." Your words have a great power to heal or to hurt.

So how much do you support people with your words? Are you an encourager or are you a discourager? Do you lift people up or do you put them down? Do you think before you speak or speak before you think?

The tongue isn't very big but it can have amazing power for good or evil; it can build up or knock down, comfort or criticise, express love or hatred, be just or judgmental, be sincere or sinister.

In a Peanuts cartoon, Peppermint Patty phones Charlie Brown and says: *"Marcie and I are about to leave for camp, Chuck. We're going to be swimming instructors."* Marcie takes the phone and adds: *"We just called to say goodbye, Charles. We are going to miss you. We love you."* Charlie Brown's little sister, Sally, asks: *"Who was that?"* Standing there by the phone with an ear-splitting grin of satisfaction on his face, Charlie Brown answers: *"I think it was a right number."*

The tongue and words can be used for good and to build others up. You can't control the tongues of others, but you can control your own. You can control what you say about another person.

Let your tongue and your words become instruments of peace, hope, inspiration, and help.

HEATHER

It was a few years later that I met her again. Heather was her name; she was a nurse who nursed me when I was in the Intensive Care Unit in hospital. I will always remember her for as I lay there helpless unable to do anything for myself; when she was there I felt so safe and confident; that if anything went wrong; everything would be alright; and what a difference that makes to someone in that situation. And I would just like to say thank you and pay tribute to all nurses; they maybe are not always aware of the comfort, courage, confidence and strength that they give to the patients at times; and they are often not thanked enough.

We can never always know the effect we are having as we go about our daily lives. Like Faithful in the Pilgrim's Progress we lift up our voice because our heart is strong and some poor soul struggling along the way is helped.

The humblest of lives are full of what perhaps could be called, unconscious ministries; words that we speak and then just forget; a smile in passing; a clasp of the hand in sympathy.

In the Book of the Acts of the Apostles we read how while in prison Paul and Silas are singing and the other prisoners heard them and that made such a difference to there lives.

As you go about your life today, remember the words you speak, the smile you give can make such a difference in the life of someone who may just need that smile today.

In his parable of the Last Judgement Jesus said: *"I'm telling the solemn truth: Whenever you did one of these things to someone overlooked or ignored, that was me—you did it to me."* (Matthew 25:40 The Message)

JUST DON'T THINK IT, SAY IT

An elderly farmer and his wife were celebrating 50 years of married life. As any farmer will tell you, life on a farm can be tough; a lot of hard work is needed and money doesn't always come easily.

This couple's children gave them a party during which lots of friends congratulated the elderly couple. They looked at old pictures, brought out old music records. The couple even danced a bit to the old, familiar music. When the party was over and all had gone home the happy couple found themselves on their own. It was a tender moment. The old farmer, who was careful with his money and even more frugal with his words, felt moved to speak.

"You know, Ma, over these 50 years, sometimes I've loved you so much that I could hardly keep from telling you." She reached for a hankie, dabbed her eyes and said: *"Thank you, Pa."*

Why are we so reluctant to let others know how we feel? Why are we often so slow to speak words that others long to hear, holding back in saying things that cry out to be said? It may be just something to do with the kind of people we are but it could make such a difference if we could change and be able to express our feelings to others.

You know the verse that says: *If with pleasure you are viewing, any work a man is doing, if you like him and you trust him, tell him now. Don't withhold the approbation, till the Parson makes oration and he lies with snowy lilies o'er his brow. For no matter how you shout it, he won't know a thing about it - for he cannot read his tombstone when he's dead.*

Today may just be the day to express how you feel and tell someone you love them.

THE BACK SEAT DRIVER

I wonder have you ever taught any of your own family or someone close to you to drive. I remember teaching Ruth, one of my daughters, to drive and the first day we went out was one of the most hair-raising I have ever experienced. The driving instructor must have been better than I was for Ruth is now a very good driver. Teaching a member of your family to drive can bring about all kinds of tensions and problems.

There is the story of a young wife who was being taught to drive by her husband; as she was making a right hand turn she stalled the car and caused a traffic jam. Looking desperately at her husband she cried: "What will I do now?"

Her husband replied: *"I don't know dear, but if you would climb over here into the back seat and allow me to take the wheel, I'm sure you will be able to figure it out."*

You see it is easy to criticise when you are in the back seat; easy to say what should be done when someone else is doing it; easy to notice the mistakes when others are making them; easy to stand in the sidelines to point out where others are going wrong when playing the game.

But didn't Jesus once say something like: *"Don't pick on people, jump on their failures, criticise their faults - unless, of course, you want the same treatment; for that critical spirit has a way of coming right back to you. Be aware and do something about what is wrong in your own life before you start to judge the lives of others."*

And maybe if we all thought about that today we wouldn't be so quick to open our mouths or point that finger and that would be a very good thing; and would work wonders in our relationships with other people.

BECOMING LIKE VICTOR

I am sure many of you have seen the television series *"One Foot in the Grave"*. Well I think I must be becoming like Victor Meldrew, for some things are starting to annoy me.

I get annoyed when I drive into a car park and find some cars that are taking up more than one space. Indeed just last week I saw one that was parked up the middle of the white line with half on one side and half on the other.

But one thing that annoys me even more is when I see perfectly fit and healthy people parking in those spaces reserved for drivers who have some disability.

Perhaps they think that what they have to do is so much more important than anyone else. Or they think that they'll only be a minute but to a person in a wheelchair, a minute can be like an hour.

I also get annoyed by cars parked up on the footpath around which elderly people and mothers pushing prams have to navigate.

So give a little thought to others; be considerate and helpful and you will show Jesus to people every day. Let's not take advantage of them.

In the letter of James in the New Testament we read these words: *What good is it, my brothers, if a man claims to have faith but has no deeds? Can such faith save him? Suppose a brother or sister is without clothes and daily food. If one of you says to him: "Go, I wish you well; keep warm and well fed," but does nothing about his physical needs, what good is it? In the same way, faith by itself, if it is not accompanied by action, is dead.* (James 2:14-17)

THE TILLEY LAMP

I must confess that I am one of those gadget people. I would love nothing better than to go out and buy all the hi-tech equipment I can find that will wash my clothes, iron my shirts, tell me what is happening on the other side of the world, deal with my accounts, play my music to annoy the neighbours, or tap in to the internet. But even if I have it all and fail to plug it into the power, it will be of no use whatsoever.

When I was young living on the farm, the electricity cables were going up the road past the end of our lane (or lonen as we called it) but my grandfather would have none of it. He said that yellow light would ruin your eyesight. And it never was put in until he died and that was some 20 years later. I remember when our first child was born we took him up to the farm. It was getting dark and the Tilley lamp was brought over to have a look at him. (To see if he was like his father or not, dear help him.)

So often it can be like that for us; the power is running past our lives, there available to us; power that could flood our lives with light and love and energy and we still go on living in the dim light of the Tilley lamp and we have no idea where we are because we cannot really see properly.

And that power! That power from on high that comes from God is available to you today.

As Paul says: *The same power that raised Jesus from the dead is available to us.*

So why not switch on to that power? Turn off the Tilley lamp and begin to experience today the real life and the real light that God has planned for you.

NEARER THAN YOU THINK

A member of the congregation took me out fishing one day and I caught 24 mackerel; but by the time I had got off the boat it had become 34 and when I walked up the pier then 44 and by the next day it had reached 84. For we all tend of exaggerate at times. When you go out fishing it's great if you catch fish but how frustrating it must have been for Peter and the others in the Gospel story who had been up all night and caught nothing; bad enough if it had only been a pastime, but for them it was their livelihood.

And in the grey dawn, they were almost on the point of giving up; when this figure from the shore shouts to them: *"Have you any fish?"* And back goes the reply: *"We have been at it all night and we have caught nothing!"*

"Cast your net on the other side, on the right side of the boat." And we all know the rest of the story.

They could hardly take on board all the fish that were caught in the nets.

There is one thing that I believe that we all need to note about this story. Simply this: that what they were looking for was nearer than they thought; indeed just within the sweep of their nets.

It's so true in life; that what we are searching for is often nearer than we think.

Success and happiness may be what you are looking for but stop, look closer! Look at your family; those who love you; the trusting voice that calls you Mammy or Daddy, Granda or Granny; what about the neighbours who hold you in high regard and affection and who know they can turn to you when they need help; think about the little things that mean so much which you often take for granted; love and security that you find within the home and family circle.

Isn't that happiness or success nearer than you think, and within your grasp? *"Cast your net on the right side of the boat."*

YOU HAVE ONLY ONE BASKET

I went shopping the other day and I thought that a basket would do. I knew what I was looking for and I thought I knew where it was but it had been moved somewhere else. They do that on you at times in the supermarkets, because then you might see something else; something else you think you might need and into the basket it goes. That is just what happened to me for those biscuits looked nice and that cake and that...... So soon the basket began to get heavier and heavier and I was either going to have to get another basket or leave something out.

So I got one of those small convenience trolleys. My grand-daughter Jemma doesn't allow her mother to use one of them, for she calls them "granny" trolleys. Granny trolley or granda trolley or not, I got one.

In a sense that is what our lives can be like; we keep on piling one thing on top of another. But the difference in our lives is that we have only got one basket, and there is only a certain amount we can carry. So you have got to decide what the things are that you need to carry in your lives. You have to decide what your priorities are and the truth is that sometimes even good things need to be declined in order to fulfil the purpose of your lives.

We need to recognise that we have got limits to what we can or cannot do.

We are human, we are feeble, we are fragile and there is a limit to what we can ask our bodies to carry and the danger comes when we ask them to carry too much.

It may be that you need to sit down today to consider your life and decide what you can do and what you are trying to do and realistically you cannot do.

To decide what your real priorities are.

Then decide to do just what you can, for remember you cannot have another basket.

MIST OVER THE MOURNES

The mist was down all around us as we made our way up the side of the Mourne Wall in our effort to climb Slieve Donard, the highest mountain in the Mournes. On and on we walked towards the summit and then it happened, about 200ft from the top we found ourselves in brilliant sunshine above the cloud level; a clear blue sky above and there below us the peaks of the other mountains showing above the mist.

It was then that I had a real sense of the might and majesty of God in all the wonder of his creation; to use the in phrase of today it was for me one of those defining moments in my life and in my faith; and not only for me but for one of the boys standing beside me who said: *"This couldn't just have happened!"*

And neither it could and neither will such an experience be yours until you are prepared to get up and get out and do something to change the situation you find yourself in at this moment. You can sit there in the mist, the mists of your despair, sorrow and disappointment or whatever the mist may be for you or you can walk on through the mist until you come to the bright blue sky and the new life and the fresh opportunities that God has prepared for you.

Could I leave you with that picture of blue sky above and the mountain peaks just showing above the mist; for you may find yourself walking through the mist at this moment and can see nothing but darkness; but if you allow God to lead you He will lead you through and lead you on into the light; to the clear blue sky and hope will shine again.

You may give up on many things in life but don't give up on God for He never gives up on you.

As the Psalmist says at the end of that 42nd Psalm: *Put your trust in God.*

Do not give up on hope.

ABOVE THE DOOR

Recently we did some renovations to our church in Dunfanaghy and I was asked to think of some suitable words to put at the entrance. After giving it some thought I always ended up coming back to the one verse, words of Jesus to his disciples, when they were under so much pressure: *"Come with me by yourselves to a quiet place and get some rest."*

They are some of my favourite words in the Bible and they are words which I have kept coming back to in my life and ministry. Words which I believe have something to say to every one of us and to everyone who will walk in through those doors. We are a people under pressure. We live lives that are continually in a hurry, with no time to do the things we want to do or should be doing. Typified in the story of the three-year-old boy who, when asked where he lived, replied: "In my car seat."

Think of your life for a moment. If you've got children, you've got school, homework, sports, extra-curricular activities, and their social life. You become a sort of private taxi firm for your children.

Then there is the home, cooking, washing, ironing and shopping which instead of getting easier is becoming more complicated. Then work, projects and deadlines and employers and employees and relationships and everything piles in on top of you. Then if you are still at school you have work, classes, homework, tests, exams, results and of course teachers and parents. On and on we could go, and we have no time for ourselves, for our families and our friends. And we begin to become weary and tired and somehow begin to skim over the important things of life.

The truth is we are never going to reach our full potential in life and relationships, mentally, physically or spiritually until we do something about the pace we try to keep up in our lives.

I think we all really take to heart those words of Jesus: *"Come with me by yourselves to a quiet place and get some rest."*(Mark 6:31 NIV)

And we all need to begin to do that today.

FROM THE INSIDE OUT

You may have heard the story of family who lived on a farm; they never had any reason to be away from the farm but on one occasion they had to go into the city. The mother went off to explore the shops while the father and the son wandered around and ended up in one of the large hotels. They were fascinated by this metal wall that opened and people got in and got out. As they watched this elderly lady came up and the wall opened and in she stepped and then it closed. They watched the numbers up above door going up 1,2,3…..then started coming down. And out stepped this lovely young woman. The father elbowed his son and said: *"Boy, go get Your Maw. I'm gonna run her through that thing one time."*

It would be great if change could take place as quickly as that; for most of us would like to change our lives for the better. That's why there are so many commercials for diet and exercise products, for skin care and anti-ageing creams as we are being encouraged by modern advertising to be 60 coming on 40. If you are really keen you can always get an injection of botox and that will take away your wrinkles for a while. We all would like to be changed for the better.

But real change for the better comes when we change ourselves not from the outside but from the inside.

A little girl was visiting her grandmother one beautiful spring morning. They walked out into grandmother's flower garden. As grandmother was inspecting the progress of her flowers, the little girl decided to try to open a rosebud with her own two hands. But no luck! As she would pull the petals open, they would tear or bruise or wilt or break off completely. Finally, in frustration, she said: *"Granny, I just don't understand it at all. When God opens a flower, it looks so beautiful but when I try, it just comes apart."* *"Well, dear,"* her Granny answered, *"There's a good reason for that. God is able to do it because He works from the inside out!"*

And that is what happened on that day of Pentecost when the Holy Spirit came the followers of Jesus were changed from the inside out.

And that is what God can do for you and for me if we ask Him and we let Him.

Then we will be really changed for the better.

JUST DON'T SIT THERE

When I read the story of Larry Walters I just couldn't believe it. It seemed so far fetched that I checked it out. When he was 33 years old Larry decided he wanted to see his neighbourhood from a new perspective. He went down to the local army surplus store one morning and bought 45 used weather balloons. That afternoon he strapped himself into a garden chair, to which several of his friends tied the now helium-filled balloons. He took along something to eat and drink, and a pellet gun, thinking he could shoot the balloons one at a time when he was ready to land.

Walters, who assumed the balloons would lift him about 100 feet in the air, was caught off guard when the chair soared almost 16,000 feet into the sky - smack into the middle of the air traffic lane at Los Angeles International Airport. Too frightened to shoot any of the balloons, he stayed airborne for more than two hours, forcing the airport to shut down its runways and causing long delays for flights from across the country.

Soon after he was safely on the ground and arrested by the police, reporters asked him three questions:

"Were you scared?" "Yes!"

"Would you do it again?" "No!"

"Why did you do it?" "Because," he answered, "you can't just sit there."

And neither can you! You cannot just sit there for the Bible tells us that God has created us for a purpose; and we can only achieve that purpose when we decide to use the life and the gifts that God has given us. Not to bury them but to take them and use them for the good of ourselves and for the good of others.

Let us all take these words of the hymn to heart.

Rise up Oh men of God, have done with lesser things, give heart and soul and mind and strength to serve the King of Kings.

So just don't sit there today but go out and make a difference and decide to make something out of your life.

Larry Walters was later fined $4,000 by the Federal Aviation Administration for violations of the Federal Aviation Act, including operating a "civil aircraft for which there is not currently in effect an airworthiness certificate" and operating an aircraft within an airport traffic area "without establishing and maintaining two-way communications with the control tower". Walters appealed, and the fine was reduced to $1,500.

BEING THERE

One minister was trying to reach out to the slum dwellers for Christ. When he first moved into this neighbourhood, he sought out a local drug dealer (to ask him why he was so successful in dragging people into his lifestyle)... and the drug dealer gave him, a lesson in why the church was losing to gangs in the battle for the souls of young people. He explained to him: *"I'm there when Johnny goes out for a loaf of bread for his mother. I'm there when he comes out of school, there when he walks the streets at night, you're not. I win, you lose, it's all about being there."*

When I read that story I remember a discussion I heard some years ago on television about being a good parent. One mother was asked what was the secret of being a good mother and she answered "Being there". Just being there!

You may not always agree with what your son or daughter has done; the mess they have made of their lives; the friends they have but it is so very important to always be there for them. That is the greatest of gifts that we could offer our children and those whom we love and which the Church should offer the people in need within our society. Just being there can make such a difference to community. When people are ill, the neighbours are there to help; when someone is in hospital they are visited; and the whole idea of the wake at the time of a funeral is based on this concept of being there. Being there is how we can make a difference to the lives of others.

As one famous rugby player was asked why he of all people should get down on the ground and hold the ball for the person who was taking the kick. *"Well,"* he said, *"if I didn't, it would fall over."*

Just think about that in relation to your life and relationships.

Recognise and understand that concept of "being there."

Our example for this is Jesus who was always there for people and who no matter who we are is still always there for us; no matter what we have done. As Paul expresses it in his letter to the Church at Philippi: *"Your attitude should be the same as that of Christ Jesus."* (Philippians 2:5: NIV)

A SOUTHERN BOY

Linda, a first year student at university was decidedly discontent with the young men who kept trying to ask her out on a date. After listening to her complaints about each one of them, her roommate offered to arrange a blind date.

"Would you prefer a southern boy or a northern boy?" she asked. "What's the difference?" Linda inquired. Her roommate explained: "Southern boys are more romantic. They will take you walking in the moonlight and whisper sweet nothings in your ear. Northern boys are more active. They like to go places and do exciting things." Linda pondered the contrast, then asked: "Could you please find me a southern boy from as far north as possible?"

We are often like Linda in our attitude to life. We often want the best of both worlds. We want what we have but we also want what others have. And life becomes an endless cycle of trying to go one better than others around us; of keeping up with the neighbours and we never become content with life as it is for we believe there is something better out there that will bring us real happiness.

Sooner or later we have got to realise that we sometimes have to accept things as they are. That we cannot always get what we want and that sometimes we have to accept the rough with the smooth. When we learn that lesson then we will learn the secret of contentment and then true fulfilment and happiness may well be ours in life.

No, we do not always get what we want but I have discovered that God quite often gives us what we need.

If you learn to accept life as it is you may well one day get that southern boy from as far north as possible.

A POCKET WITH HOLES

An old absent minded bachelor; that's what the village folk called the local Presbyterian minister, the Rev Ninian McLachlan.

One day he met one of his more pious elders on the road and hurriedly stuffed his lighted pipe into his pocket and forget about it; until he discovered that it had burned a hole right through the inside lining.

Some days later he met a gardening friend who gave him a spare packet of nasturtium seeds. Don't sow them until the first week in May he was told; and he put the packet into his pocket.

Ah yes, the first week in May, he kept reminding himself. But with the constant rumble of his hand in and out of his pocket; the bag burst unbeknown to him and as he walked around his parish, two or three seeds every now and then dropped out of his pocket.

About the end of May the absent minded minister remembered about the seeds; he put his hand in, brought out the packet but there were no seeds left.

"Ah well!" he said, with a saving touch of humour. I'll have helped at least to brighten up my parish."

Then the miracle took place; that parish blazed with splashes of yellow, scarlet and golden nasturtium flowers in the most astonishing corners, in the hedgerows and in the ditches and by the wayside..

Is it not true that what the world needs today is people like the Rev Ninian McLachlan with holes in their pockets from which the seeds of love and joy may fall to brighten up this somewhat sad, confused and mixed-up world? People like you....people like me...

So that some day, somewhere, somehow, someone will come to learn of God's love and forgiveness because of the seeds that have fallen from our lives as we have passed by.

TAILPIECES

Here is a little poem that I read at a recent concert in Letterkenny and many have asked to hear it again. But let us not only hear it but act upon it in our lives. I have no idea who the author is.

FRIENDS

Around the corner I have a friend,
In this great city that has no end,
Yet the days go by and weeks rush on,
And before I know it, a year is gone.

And I never see my old friend's face,
For life is a swift and terrible race,
He knows I like him just as well,
As in the days when I rang his bell.

And he rang mine but we were younger then,
And now we are busy, tired men.
Tired of playing a foolish game,
Tired of trying to make a name.

"Tomorrow" I say! "I will call on Jim,
Just to show that I'm thinking of him."
But tomorrow comes and tomorrow goes,
And distance between us grows and grows.

Around the corner, yet miles away,
"There's a message sir - Jim died today."
And that's what we get and deserve in the end,
Around the corner, a vanished friend.

PARABLE OF IMMORTALITY

by Henry Van Dyke

I am standing upon the seashore. A ship at my side spreads her white sails to the morning breeze and starts for the blue ocean. She is an object of beauty and strength, and I stand and watch until at last she hangs like a speck of white cloud just where the sea and sky come down to mingle with each other. Then someone at my side says: "There she goes!"

Gone where? Gone from my sight ... that is all. She is just as large in mast and hull and spar as she was when she left my side and just as able to bear her load of living freight to the place of destination. Her diminished size is in me, not in her. And just at the moment when someone at my side says: "There she goes! There are other eyes watching her coming and other voices ready to take up the glad shout: "Here she comes!"

The Easter message proclaims that death is but the horizon over which we pass to that new and fuller life with God. Therein is to be found the hope of life anew.

Take Time to Pray (Author unknown)

I got up early one morning
And rushed right into the day;
I had so much to accomplish
I didn't take time to pray.

Problems just tumbled about me
And heavier grew each task;
Why doesn't God help me, I wondered.
He answered: "You didn't ask."

I wanted to see joy and beauty,
But the day toiled on, grey and bleak;
I wondered why God didn't show me --
He said: "But you didn't seek."

I tried to come into God's presence;
I used all my keys at the lock;
God gently and lovingly chided:
"My child, you didn't knock."

I woke up early this morning
And paused before entering the day;
I had so much to accomplish
That I had to take time to pray.

So take time to pray today.....

HIGHLAND INSPIRATION

The Highland Inspiration committee gratefully acknowledges the assistance of the following sponsors, without whose support this publication would not have been possible. Thanks to their generosity, the costs of producing the book have been covered, which means that all the proceeds from sales will go to Donegal Hospice.

Kirk Session, congregational committee and members of Carrigart Presbyterian Church.

Kirk Session, congregational committee and members of Dunfanaghy Presbyterian Church.

Frank & Hilary Casey, Rosapenna Hotel.

Will Chambers, W&J Chambers, Drumahoe.

Roger Currie, Modern Office Supplies, Belfast.

Jim Deeney, National Irish Bank, Dublin.

Patrick J Doherty, PJD Contractors, Coshclady, Bunbeg.

John & Barbara Eakin, Portnablagh.

Maud Gray, Portnablagh.

Willie & Mary Hogg, Belfast.

Drew Hunter, Cashel, Creeslough.

Tom & Sheila Hunter, Waringstown.

The Lord Kilclooney, Alpha Newspapers, Moygashel.

Tom & Joy Killick, Bangor.

John & Wendy Lyons, Drumbo, Lisburn.

Manus McFadden, MTM Fireplaces, Creeslough.

John & Jennifer McLarnon, Portnablagh.

Arthur McMahon, Donegal Oil, Letterkenny.

Peter McNutt, McNutt's, Downings.

Gale & Helen Moffett, Newtownards.

Edmund Moore, Dunfanaghy.

Marshall & Margaret Moore, Randalstown.

Charlie & Mary Robinson, Portnablagh.

Ernest Stewart, Kerrykeel, Milford.

Photo: Stanley Matchett

Bunbeg Harbour

Photo: Sammy Wasson

Trá Na Rosann beach on The Atlantic Drive

Photo: Stanley Matchett

Evening Sunset - Bunbeg

Photo: Stanley Matchett

Doe Castle - Creeslough

Magheraoarty Beach

Glenveagh Castle and National Park

Derryveagh

Photo: Sammy Wasson

Take time to wonder

Photo: Stanley Matchett